Creating Resilience:

Ego Strengthening Hypnosis Scripts

Scripts to Enhance and Strengthen Self-Concept and Create Desired Client Outcomes Using Hypnosis and Neurolinguistic Programming

By Cindy Locher, BCH, MNLP

Creating Resilience: Ego Strengthening Hypnosis Scripts

ISBN 978-1-304-76365-5

Copyright 2014 Cindy Locher, BCH

All Rights Reserved. No part of this publication may be reproduced in any form or by any means, including scanning, photocopying, or otherwise, without prior written permission of the policyholder.

Disclaimer and Terms of Use: The Author has striven to be as accurate and complete as possible in the creation of this book, notwithstanding the fact that she does not warrant or represent at any time that the contents within are complete due to the rapidly changing nature of the world. While all attempts have been made to verify information provided in this publication, the Author and Publisher assume no responsibility for errors, omissions, or contrary interpretation of the subject matter herein. Any perceived slights of specific persons, peoples or organizations are unintentional. In practical advice books, like anything else in life, there are no guarantees of outcomes. Readers are cautioned to rely on their own judgement about their individual circumstances and to act accordingly. This book is not intended for use as a source of medical or counseling advice. All readers are advised to seek the services of competent professionals in the medical or mental health fields, as deemed necessary.

~Dedications~

For my Dad, who raised me with hypnosis. I'll always remember my Dad saying, when I was about 10 years old, "Never start by telling yourself no. You may find out as you move forward that the world shows you a different answer than what you expected, but never start by telling yourself no." Dad, your words have always gone with me. Wish you were here.

~~~

For my husband, Dan, who has been the most supportive and amazing soul mate I could have ever imagined. Thank you for being in my life!

For my daughter, Grace, who is the brightest light shining in my world. I love who you've been, who you are, and who you will become!

Special thanks to everyone in my "hypnosis family" who have always encouraged me, inspired me, and shown me a path even as I've forged my own. Too many to be named!

~Acknowledgements~

To say that one has written something by oneself is hubris. I'd like to acknowledge all of the inspirational content that my subconscious mind has absorbed, with and without my conscious intent, which has resulted in the scripts in this book. Consciously, my chief influences in script writing have been Wendi Friesen, the late Barrie Konikov, and Mark Tyrrell, but I'm certain that many other influences are at work here as well.

Undying thanks to all of my teachers, too many to name, to my students (I often think you teach me more than I do you!) and to my "partner in crime" at ChangeWorks Hypnosis Center & the Midwest Hypnotherapy Academy, Jody Kimmell, CHt.

Table of Contents

Introduction 6

Part 1: Scripts for Personal Change

Create Readiness for Change 9

Transform Your Past 13

Restoring Personal Power 19

The Unbreakable Self 22

Master of All Decisions 31

No Failure, Just Feedback 37

Totem of Confidence & Power 43

Fuel Your Fire 48

Part 2: Scripts for Weight Release and Healthier Habits

Eliminate Sugar 51

Hypno Diet Pill 57

Nighttime Weight Release 63

Natural Weight Release 70

Confidence for Weight Release 79

Table of Contents, Continued

Part 3: Scripts for Improving Libido

Drive Your Desire 85

Passion: A Burning Desire 89

Part 4: Scripts for Improved Health & Stress Reduction

Cindy's Progressive Relaxation 91

Deep Healing & Cellular Release 93

Introduction

This volume of scripts is the result of several years of client and recording work, and reflects my personal experience and growing philosophy of changework. These scripts combine concepts and often patterns from Neurolinguistic Programming with traditional hypnosis script patter, as I find NLP utilized in trance to be highly effective for my clients.

You will find that the first section, Scripts for Personal Change, is the largest and most complete section. This follows my belief and experience that most of the presenting issues that people come for help with are symptoms of an underlying, unresolved issue, either from the past or present. While clients come expecting suggestions to perhaps, drink more water, eat less food, or feel distanced and separated from their undesired habit, the underlying foundations of personal resilience, ego strengthening, and mental flexibility must be addressed and improved, the past released and underlying emotional scars healed, in order for changes to be lasting in nature.

This volume does not contain scripts or processes for uncovering Initial Sensitizing Events or unresolved issues underlying symptomatic behaviors, but rather focuses on strengthening the self. If you are not educated and practiced in the areas of ISE discovery and release, your effectiveness as a hypnotist or hypnotherapist will be compromised. I whole heartedly recommend books and trainings from C. Roy Hunter for a strong foundation in the art of hypnotherapy. In addition, myself and my partner Jody L. Kimmell, CHt, teach an advanced and expanded hypnotherapy certification curriculum at our school in Minnesota, the Midwest Hypnotherapy Academy, and we are available to field your questions and receive your comments.

A word on script delivery.
Hypnosis script delivery is a unique form of vocal performance, quite unlike any other form of spoken word delivery. For years now, I've had a radio show, which serves as an example on the other end of the spectrum. When you are on the radio, you learn that when people have only your voice to hold their attention, that your vocal delivery needs to be MORE dynamic than other types of presentations. Your on air

performance demands more variation in tone, volume, range, and of course complete avoidance of pauses--the dreaded "dead air." Delivery of a hypnosis script is the complete opposite, and your effectiveness will increase as the "interest value" of your delivery decreases. I encourage you to play with slowing your pace, dropping your voice into a lower register, flattening out the dynamic elements of your delivery into more of a monotone and employing extended pauses. I am not as monotone in my delivery as some; my inflection still conveys emotion, but if you compared my hypnosis delivery to the playful dynamics of, say, reading a children's book, you'll see a definite difference. Don't be afraid to pause, even for what seems like a long period, allowing the client's mind to process and create its own meanings from the words you deliver. You'll notice that the session, "Cindy's Progressive Relaxation," is a very short script in terms of the number of words, but has explicit instructions to plan out the delivery to last fifteen minutes. If you're uncomfortable with pauses and slowing your delivery, practicing delivering this script and timing it out to fifteen minutes will help to train you to be comfortable with the slow, gentle, drawn out delivery of a hypnosis script.

Likewise, some of these scripts are quite long, and depending on the induction method you prefer, may require 30, 40 minutes or more to delivery appropriately. Be sure to plan your client session times accordingly.

A script is a framework.

These scripts should be used as a reference and framework for your client work. Every person is different, even if they seem to have similar presenting issues. These scripts provide ideas and jumping off points. When you have the luxury of working directly with someone, you also have the responsibility to use your training and abilities to tailor your approach custom to them. That said, everyone uses inspiration and the ideas of others that have come before them, whether they acknowledge that consciously, or not. There is quite a bit of debate out there amongst hypnotists on the subject of scripts, and you'll find every position represented, from "always use scripts" to "never use scripts," and of course the positions in between.

My own opinion is that scripts are useful to prime your mind with new ideas, and to keep the work fresh for you as a hypnotist. Any hypnotist with years of experience behind them has read, listened to, or been exposed to in some way, to thousands of scripts. Because those scripts, that language or patter, is important to them, their subconscious mind has filed away and cataloged all of it. So even when a hypnotist is "anti-script" and believes they don't make use of them, the influence of those scripts is still being used in the spontaneous creation of the language they are using with their clients. That is my belief.

Use these scripts to continue to build your own repertoire, your own mental library of material upon which to draw. Always honor your client by familiarizing yourself with the script as it pertains to them and addresses their issue, and altering and customizing the script for that particular individual.

Some of these scripts were transcribed from live client sessions. After those sessions I felt that what had come forth from my subconscious mind had enough universal appeal to be helpfully applied to others. Some of these scripts were written specifically to be recorded in studio for products. You will find a strong NLP influence in these scripts, as I am both a Master Hypnotist and a Master NLP Practitioner, and have been combining both approaches clinically for years. I personally believe that the inclusion of NLP concepts and patterns is enhanced by being applied within the hypnotic state.

How you may use these scripts.

These scripts are provided in this format for your direct use with clients, as a reference and framework. You have permission to deliver these scripts orally to your clients as part of your session work. You may record these scripts as part of your session(s) for a particular client(s) personal use only. You may not record, sell, republish or otherwise represent these scripts as your own in any way without express written permission by the author.

It is my deepest wish that these scripts help you to create lasting, positive change with your clients!

Part 1: Scripts for Personal Change

Create Readiness for Change

About the script:

I wrote this script after a fruitless search for script patter to help people, not with a specific change, but to prepare their minds for a desired change. To create fertile ground, so to speak. Occassionally I find that clients come to me feeling that they are ready for the results of the change they desire, but not really prepared for what change entails in terms of the ecology of their lives and the energy of change itself. Even when change is initiated and produced at the subconscious level, it requires energy to change.

It would be well to have a conversation with the client or to assign homework around the ecology of change, and have a discussion about the cycle of change with your client prior to or in conjunction with conducting this session. Questions to facilitate discussion and thought around the ecology of change are provided below. The model of personal change that I find works best for discussing with clients is the model created by Kris and Tim Halbom of NLP of California, "The Universal Cycles of Change."

Ecology of change questions: If I could have it now, would I take it? Are all costs and consequences of achieving your outcome, including the time involved, acceptable to you and anyone else affected by it?

This is known as ecology. Consider the costs, consequences, environmental and third party impact of having the outcome. This can be done in a dialogue but is an excellent written or journaling exercise that can be done over the course of several days prior to a session.

I have recorded this session and often provide it to clients who are deciding whether or not they are ready to commit to doing sessions for changework. If, for example, a smoker is at say a "7" on a scale of 1 to 10 for feeling motivated to do the work, then I'll provide them with this recording (and probably some other homework as well) and schedule a time to discuss in a week or two and re-evaluate their readiness to do the work of change.

Script: Create Readiness for Change

USE YOUR PREFERRED INDUCTION METHOD

Before you move more deeply into hypnosis, begin by doing a little honest self-evaluation. You want the change, yes, you want the RESULT. But you realize that making a meaningful change in your life will require you to change. To do things differently. To make different choices. To be strong in the face of old desires and triggers. To a lesser degree because you're using hypnosis to make the change easier, but regardless, having not gone through this change, there is a part of you that fears how strong those triggers might be. Acknowledging this fear is an important step on your path to change and growth.

So, take the time, just before each session, to do this honest, self evaluation. And watch how it changes day by day as your readiness to move through the change process grows stronger. It's easy to do. Just ask yourself, on a scale of 1 to 10, 10 being totally ready to commit to and make the change I want, where I am I on that scale right now?

After listening to this recording, ask yourself that same question again.

You will know when it's time to put this recording away as you will have already begun making the changes you desire.

Repeat the following in your mind, silently but strongly:

I am ready for change and I am ready to change.

I realize there is a gap, a difference, between how I have been, and how I can be, want to be, deserve to be and am becoming.

I am now focusing on how I am becoming, the new me that is coming into expression.

I recognize the behaviors that have held me back in the past. Whether those are old habits, excuses, rationalizations, attitudes or beliefs.

I love myself enough to create this change in my behaviors and in my reality; in how I AM. I realize that sometimes, self love is tough love. I will no longer turn a blind eye or excuse the behaviors that have held me back in the past.

When I make excuses for self limiting behavior, I now recognize those excuses for what they are. I sweep all excuses aside and I MAKE A NEW CHOICE FOR MYSELF NOW.

I recognize rationalizing for what is it. I sweep aside all rationalizations or justifications and I MAKE A NEW CHOICE FOR MYSELF NOW.

I clearly see old habits as simply old choices that have been made over and over. I realize that at one point, that choice that is now a habit was once a new choice. This gives me further evidence that I CAN make new choices, and I MAKE A NEW CHOICE FOR MYSELF NOW.

When I express old attitudes or beliefs that kept me tied to the old me, I will hear them clearly and know them for what they are. I allow old attitudes and beliefs that are not beneficial to becoming the new me to simply fade and disappear as I MAKE NEW CHOICES FOR MYSELF NOW.

The best teachers are the teachers who see what we can become and what we are capable of, and who pull that out of us despite our own hesitations or doubts. Who insist on higher standards, greater performance from us even when we don't believe we are capable of achieving those standards, and who stand by us with a knowing smile when we surprise ourselves with the heights of our abilities. I NOW BECOME MY OWN BEST TEACHER.

As I focus on who I am becoming, I can feel my choices changing, my mind growing stronger, my self esteem increasing and my love for myself expanding every day.

As I focus on who I am becoming, I realize that big changes are made up of lots of little changes. I make little changes every day, and each day I make more little changes that lead me to my goal. I find power in adding up all the little changes and accepting and appreciating that the journey to the result is a necessary and self-building (self affirming?) part of becoming the new me. I know, on a deep level, that the little changes and choices, each and every moment of decision, makes the end result, that new ME that I desire, even more permanent and precious.

I realize that when I reach my goal, I will have changed. Not just on the surface, but inside, in the way I think, the way I feel about myself, others, life and the world around me. I respect and acknowledge that the old me, the me that I'm leaving behind, was not bad or wrong. It is simply that I have made a choice to grow.

I now clearly see that all of my life is a result of choices that I have made in the past. Those choices were the right choices for that time in my life, but I am no longer that person. I choose now to grow, to become the new me that I have conceived of in my mind. This is my choice, and my choice alone, and because I love myself and because I am now my own best teacher, I grow stronger and more fully expressed in who I am each and every day.

Take some time now in silence and allow your mind to integrate, for your best and highest good, the beneficial suggestions you have just received.

Exit trance in your preferred manner.

Transform Your Past

About the script

This script is designed to transmute the negative energies of the past into their pure form as energy only, allowing the energy to be transformed into something beneficial. In this way the client's mind can acknowledge that the events happened, but energetically shift those events and their meanings in a way that is in keeping with their highest and best expressions and conceptions of self.

Script: Transform Your Past

USE YOUR PREFERRED INDUCTION METHOD

And just relax. Picture, visualize, imagine or just pretend that you are standing at the top of a staircase of ten steps. A very safe, very secure, well lit staircase. This is a very special staircase and it's special for a number of reasons. The first reason it's special is because it's yours. This is your staircase just as this is your experience in hypnosis. So make the staircase what you want it to be. You might choose to accept what first shows up for you. Or you might decide to change it. To carpet the stairs in your favorite color. To make it more grand or more simple. To hang up a chandelier, a light fixture that you enjoy. Good. This is your special staircase. Another reason the staircase is special is because every step down this staircase is going to relax you even more completely. Relaxing your body, relaxing your mind, every step down the staircase will take you to a deeper place where it's more still and calm, quiet. And before we start down the staircase ask your subconscious mind to choose for you a symbol or an image that represents your goal of releasing the negatives from your past, releasing any limiting beliefs, behaviors or other obstacles that were created as a result of those interactions that you may have had at a younger age or at any previous time in your life up to the present day.

The first symbol, the first image that pops into you mind is the right one. Even if it doesn't make any sense to your subconscious mind at all. The first image that pops into your mind when ask for an image that represents your goal, that's the one. Place it at the bottom of the staircase so it is waiting for you. And so the staircase is now special because every step down the staircase brings you closer to reaching that goal. So let's begin stepping down the staircase as I count backwards from ten, nine, eight, deeper or deeper down, seven, try imagining the feeling of the stair beneath your step. Feel it. Six, five, or the handrail beneath your hand, feel the texture of it, the smoothness, the temperature. Four, down, and down, three, everything slowing down for you, becoming more still and calm, more quiet and relaxed. One and zero. Zero. Zero is deep sleep. Deep sleep. And at zero you have reached that symbol, that image, that goal. You have reached that goal so claim it for yourself. Whatever makes sense to you, claim that goal as your own. And do that now. Good. When you have claimed that goal for yourself, let me know by lifting the index finger of your left hand.

Good. And understand something very important about hypnosis, that you are in a place now where you are truthful and honest with yourself. So the fact that your subconscious mind allowed you to claim that goal means that your subconscious mind sees that goal as an appropriate goal for you, as a goal that will bring benefits into your life. And as a goal that is achievable. And once your subconscious mind accepts a goal as appropriate beneficial and achievable it becomes your ally. The most powerful ally you could ask for in turning that goal into reality. So just relax now. Relax and allow your subconscious mind to do all the work. Because it's your ally now. It knows exactly what you desire. And all you need to do is relax and go deeper.

Deeper down as I count from five down to zero allowing, imagining or just pretending that every number from five down to zero represents an even deeper state of hypnosis. Starting with five, and drifting down, four, three, two, one, zero. Zero is deep sleep. And anytime I count from five down to zero and say the words deep sleep with your permission and the purpose of hypnosis, you will reach this level of hypnosis or deeper quickly and easily.

Now, your only job is to relax, relaxing more completely with every breath, with every word that I say that every sound that you hear, with every thought or idea that crosses your mind. Relax and allow your subconscious mind to do all the work for you. Because you're subconscious mind has already accepted that goal and your subconscious mind knows amazing, creative, inventive ways to achieve that goal for you. So you can simply relax.

And now ask your subconscious mind to revisit all of your memories from the past, all of your interactions. With your parents, your father, your son and many, many others in your past. And your subconscious mind can do this in the blink of an eye. And it revisits all of these memories, whether you are consciously aware of any of them or not, you direct your subconscious mind now to separate the good from the negative. Keeping the wisdom. Separating the wheat from the chaff, extracting or removing anything that in the past that was considered negative. The negative meaning that was previously attached to those memories by a younger you. And allow your subconscious mind to keep the positive the wisdom, the learning, the life experience of each and all of these memories. All of the wisdom, the learning, the life experience that allows you to be more effective in your life both now and in your future, all of that is yours to keep.

And as your mind looks at all of these memories, all the way back to the day you were born through the eyes of wisdom, the eyes of experience, the eyes of the adult you, your mind accepts and realizes on all levels that the negatives that previously were attached to these memories were the conclusions of a younger you. And that you are no longer that person. And that person, that younger you is no longer who you are. And that those negative meanings are no longer appropriate for you now and they are no longer appropriate for the future you. They are no longer appropriate in light of the goal that you have now accepted for yourself on all levels.

So allow yourself, your subconscious mind to separate that negative energy and then transmute it, transforming it into its true form. Simply energy. Neutral energy. It is the energy of potential, it is neither negative nor positive, it is simply the pure energy of potential. And by doing this all negative associations become completely removed from that energy released. The negative energy released from the memories and you therefore are released from the negative energy in totality.

Now direct your subconscious mind, ask your subconscious mind to transmute and transform that energy into its pure basic form. The energy of potential. You can see it as a light, or however it's right for you. Perhaps a ball of energy or a seed. Imagine taking that energy as it shifts and transmutes into that form of pure energy potential, neither positive nor negative. But having the potential to become, the potential to become. And with your direction it has the potential to become something beautiful, viable, and vibrant in the world. So imagine taking it and burying it in the mother earth just like you would a seed and watch it as it grows, blooms and matures into a beautiful, mature, magnificent and protecting tree. Strong and ancient. Imagine that tree, now see it. Feel it, experience it in any way is right for you. Perhaps you can hear the wind in the leaves of that tree or hear the bird's song of all of the birds that find shelter in its branches. Or the rustle of leaves from the squirrels leaping from brand to branch. Maybe you even see them. And as you look around the base of the tree under its beautiful spreading canopy you see that there is even more life here. This tree represents beauty and the potential of energy. To be positive to bring vital life giving forces into this world.

And it becomes a symbol for you of how things can be transformed as you remember that the energy that previously was this tree had in the past been interpreted as negative energy in your mind. Had been interpreted as negative energy attached to those old memories, those old interactions. And now you see the truth that that energy was only the energy of potential and that now is being used for a positive potential. Good.

Spend some time under this tree. Reach out and hug it. Wrap your arms around its trunk, feel the roughness of the bark. Smell it, smell the smell of the wood, the scent of the leaves, the earthy scent of the loam that it is growing in. The beautiful smell of soil. Warm and life giving. Walk around it, reach up and tough the leaves, hang and swing on a branch like a child. Lie on the ground beneath it and look up through the leaves and see the dappled sky and the sun shining down and feel the amazing, amazing energy of this tree. And allow your mind to weave back and forth like an amazing tapestry. All of the interpretations and the meanings represented to you by this tree. Good.

Now, take a talisman from this tree, an acorn, a seed, a leaf, a piece of the bark, whatever you choose. Something that represents to you all of the positive energy and all of the potential represented by this tree and the beauty of that process of transforming, of transmuting. The amazing power presented by that. And this seed, this acorn, this leaf, whatever talisman you have chosen also represents to you the ability to move forward in life in the way that you desire. In a way that reflects and honors that goal that you claimed for yourself and that your subconscious mind is now your powerful ally in achieving. And see yourself moving into the future with the ability to interpret all interactions, all relationships in a way that serves you. In a way that respects and honors your highest good in this world, your connection to the creator that honors your spirit and the spirit of the person that you are interacting with. And see yourself moving forward with that talisman. Perhaps you keep it somewhere on you know you will know that it will always be in your heart perhaps. Do whatever feels good and feels right to you. Knowing that it is now and forever here with you, giving you always this ability to see the good in people, to really look right straight through to the soul as though your higher spirit is connecting with the higher spirit of the person you are talking to. Allowing you to have conversations at multiple levels with the people in your life. And see that changing the relationships in your life in amazing and wonderful ways. Truly a force for good.

Good. Take these feelings, these images and allow yourself to move even deeper down with five, four, three, two, one, zero. Zero. Zero is deep sleep, deep sleep. And anytime I count from five down to zero and say those words deep sleep with our permission and the purpose of hypnosis you will reach this level of hypnosis or deeper quickly and easily.

Take a moment now and allow all the work that you have done today, the perfect work of your creative, intuitive, intelligent subconscious mind, allow this beautiful work to become integrated across all levels of your body, your mind and your spirit. Good.

You have done excellent work today. In a moment I am going to count from one to five and on the count of five you will return feeling rested, refreshed, full of energy, ready for the rest of our day. Tonight when you choose to sleep you will fall asleep quickly and easily and you will sleep deeply and soundly throughout the night, waking in the morning feeling rested and refreshed, feeling full of energy. Positive and happy. Right now it's time to begin the trip back starting the count up at one, returning to this time and this place, at two feeling positive energy flowing throughout your body, three, needing a little more oxygen, taking that deep breath in. Good. Four and five eyes open wide awake. One, two three, four five. Eyes open wide open, feeling great.

Restoring Personal Power

About the script

This script is another one that is helpful in restoring or moving a person toward a feeling of being "at cause" in their lives rather than "at effect." The script is written for a client who feels they can identify a person or persons to whom they've given over their personal power. If a specific person can't be identified, but still the client feels that they aren't in a position of personal power and decision in their lives, ask their subconscious mind to create a composite or proxy for the person or persons that they have given their power to in the past, or in the present. If more than one person is identified by the client, the pertinent parts of the script can be repeated with each subsequent person identified, as time allows, or multiple sessions can be done.

If you are familiar with cord cutting, that is another metaphor that can be combined with this script or used in a separate session to complement this script, as you see fit.

Script: Restoring Personal Power

USE YOUR PREFERRED INDUCTION METHOD

Take a few moments to settle into your sanctuary. Breathe in the clear, peaceful air. That's it, continue to relax and let go. As you settle in more deeply, allow your inner awareness to expand with each breath. Please stay open to the guidance and loving support that exists on this journey. Allow your intuition to "hear" and "see" your personal messages.

Move back in time now to a scene in which you gave your power to someone else. (Pause) Moving as far back as you need to go as I count from five back to one. Five... four... that's it, drifting back... three... two... and one... You're right there now at a scene from your past. Are you indoors or outdoors? Are you alone or is someone with you? Notice the details in your scene. The colors and textures. Create a safe, protected area for this meeting. You may want to bathe this area with soft yellow light. Now, ask the person to whom you gave your power to join you and thank him or her for coming. Explain that the purpose of this meeting is have your power returned.

Make your request in a very firm, self-assured and confident voice. (Pause) Put your hand out with the clear knowledge that your power is about to be returned. (Pause) If necessary, repeat your request and insist that it happen right now. (Pause) It's time to take back your personal power. (Pause) Ask for it back. Ask firmly and strongly because the power belongs to you. (Pause) Now that you have it back, hold on to it.

What does your personal power look like? What size is it? (Pause) What color? (Pause) What shape does your power take? (Pause) Does it have an aroma? (Pause) A sound? (Pause) Perhaps a texture? (Pause) Be with your power. (Pause) Feel your power! (Pause) Thank the other person now and ask them to leave. They no longer have any power over you.

Go back to your special, safe place and let all the energy of your power flow through your entire body, circulating through every cell, in every muscle, nerve and tendon. It's yours forever!

The easiest way to re-absorb your power is with your breath. Breathe your power in with each inhalation until it's completely absorbed. Breathe all the way down into your belly, that's it, deep, full breaths.

(Pause 30 sec)

I'd like you to take a look now, at your life with this power in place. Imagine a scene where you felt powerless recently. On the count of three you'll be right there at that recent scene. One... two... three... You're right there now, on the edge of that scene. Notice your interaction in this scene, without your personal power. (Pause) Now step into the scene and into that body, taking your newly recovered power with you. Go to the beginning of the scene and move through the event again, this time with your personal power. (Pause) What's different this time? (Pause) Are you different? Are the others different? (Pause) Does the outcome change? (Pause) Notice every detail about this scene. (Pause) How do your relationships change when you feel your power? (Pause) What have you learned in this process of asking for and using your personal power? (Pause)

Let your scene go now and return to your private place for a moment. If there's anything that you need right now to feel complete with this journey, take a moment to bring that in. (Pause)

Let's move forward in time now so you can see and feel this power working in your life. See or sense yourself on a beautiful path now. A path lined with colorful flowers and abundant growth. As you move along this path you are moving forward in time. Moving to a time in your future when your power is fully developed. To a point in time when you are comfortable with your power. (Pause) It's very easy now to access this future scene. Simply continue to move along this path and, as you turn the next corner, you're right there. Notice your surroundings on this path. (Pause) Are you alone or is someone with you? (Pause) You may find yourself in a familiar place, or in an entirely new place. (Pause) Notice now what your life is like with this power. (Pause) How do you feel about yourself? (Pause) How do you feel and act towards others? (Pause) Notice how differently they respond to you with your newly uncovered power. (Pause) How do you act with this new power? (Pause) Get a sense now of the joy and satisfaction that this power brings into your life. (Pause)

Now, if it feels safe and comfortable, step into that future self. See and sense what it's like to be in that future body. (Pause) Even though you may still listen to other's thoughts and feelings about your life you're now paying close attention to your own feelings and knowing what is your truth. Thank your future self and drift back, now into your private sanctuary. Breathe in all this new information and take a moment to rest. (Pause)

In a moment I'll count from one to five...on the count of five you'll return from this relaxed state feeling wonderful on every level. One... feeling the energy flowing into your arms and legs... two... feeling more and more alert with each number... three... mentally and physically refreshed... four... sleeping soundly and peacefully tonight... and five! wide awake and alert, take a deep breath and stretch!

Follow up the session with this exercise:
When you need answers or advice, first gather information from "out there" then enter the silence of meditation or self hypnosis. What action or solution does your inner voice suggest?

Describe to yourself the inner feelings that surface as you give yourself this advice. That is your personal power.

The Unbreakable Self: Personal Resilience

About the script

I became very interested in the psychological quality of resilience a few years ago. It seemed to me that it was a key personality trait of people who both are, and who *feel*, successful in their lives. Resilience, according to the American Psychology Association, is the "ability to adapt well in the face of adversity, trauma, tragedy, threats, and from sources of stress such as work pressures, health, family or relationship problems." This quality has been associated with individuals who handle crises effectively, and are able to recover and get back on their feet more quickly. Their minds seem to put events into perspective more quickly than some.

Again, after a search for existing hypnotic patter material, I found none directly addressing this other than the usual ego strengthening scripts, such as the Hartland script. Those scripts would make excellent companions to this one.

I feel this type of work is appropriate to anyone, and of course you'll use your judgement as to how and with whom to incorporate this work.

Script: The Unbreakable Self: Personal Resilience

USE YOUR PREFERRED INDUCTION METHOD

Picture yourself floating effortlessly in a calm peaceful space. This space is the center of your being, it is where all of your most important decisions, actions and thoughts are created. You are the master of this space, the one who makes all the decisions that affect your life. Within this space you have absolute power and control over what happens, you have the power to create and change anything you wish. Take one deep breath and feel the clear pure air fill your lungs, acknowledge that this place is created for you and by you. Take a moment and simply absorb the immense and ultimate power you have all around you and deep inside of you. Within this space, you are about to create a circle of excellence; a circle of color and light and power that will always be with you, from this time on, whether you are consciously aware of it or not. This circle of excellence will automatically engage your personal resilience, all of your abilities to overcome obstacles, to engage resources both within and without, to find and create solutions to any problems and to feel supported by hope and personal strength. So, let's begin.

WAIT 5 SECONDS

In front of you, begin to picture all the people who are important in your life; your family, your friends, your lover, your associates, anyone who has significant impact on your life and emotions. Some of these people may have left this plane, but their energies are still with you. See their faces in detail, see how they are looking right back at you with a gentle smile painted across their faces. Feel their intentions, how they wish to see you succeed in everything you do, how they are there for you when you are weak, and how they give you strength to overcome any adversity in your way. As you look at them begin to notice a warm gentle ray of pure energy coming from them to you. As the ray touches your chest you begin to feel how your soul bubbles with excitement, how your energy levels rise and how your confidence becomes ever more powerful. These people are your pillars of support, they are the people who will guide you through any and all hard times. These are the people that help you become the best version of you possible. As they look at you with love in their hearts and a gentle smile on their face, look back at them and thank them for being there. They chose to be with you, they love to be with you and only want to see you succeed. that is why collectively they are sending you this positive energy in the form of a warm and gentle ray. It is the reason why your soul becomes overjoyed when they are in your presence. Take a few moments to simply thank them and accept their warm gentle energy deep into your life. Make it as real as you can and anchor this feeling deep within your spirit and mind. This memory you are creating will be a powerful tool used to defeat any and all adversity that might come your way.

WAIT 5 SECONDS

As you continue to feel the energy being poured into your life, your heart and your being, simply move your loved ones slightly to your right. As they all move to the right of you a new picture emerges in front of you. This image appearing right in front of you is one of a dark nature. It is all the crises that you have suffered and gone through throughout your life. It is all present crises and those that are to come. Notice the dark aura around this picture. At first, it might <u>seem like</u> something that cannot be overcome. Now, simply look to the right and notice that your friends and family are still smiling, they are still sending you the positive vibrations. Know that regardless of any crises, past, present or future, your family and friends will always be by your side. You can still see that warm gentle ray of pure energy come your way. As you look once again at the dark image, you begin to see it fading, breaking up, becoming in some way less substantial as you realize that you have moved through and overcome obstacles and crises in your past. As you ponder this, the image begins to change. Now, realize that your family and friends are now sending a second ray of light, but not towards you, but rather towards image of darkness. As the beam of light touches that image, you can suddenly feel the power of the crises fade. You realize that this is merely a temporary energy, it has no permanent place in your life. The more you realize this truth the weaker the dark being becomes and the stronger you become. Your family and friends, your circle of confidence is helping you to overcome any and all obstacles in your life and changing the color of this dark being's ray of light. Instead of being a dark grey beam of light, it is turning into a wonderful blue and calming beam hitting you right in the head., and a feeling of reassurance fills you. This newly changed beam of light begins to tell your mind how you can overcome any adversity, how you can solve any problem. It is teaching you how to outlive and outdo any obstacle presented to you. With the help of your circle of confidence you become stronger, even more powerful than before. You begin to change the image of this dark being. Make it small and weak something that you can easily defeat. You are more powerful than any obstacle that might come your way. Take this knowledge and anchor it deep inside your mind and body. Know that you are never alone and that any problem is not a problem, just a hidden solution. You hold the keys to all your solutions, to all your victories. The dark being becomes small and easily defeated. Know that no matter how big an obstacle might seem, by breaking it into smaller bite size solutions, by enlisting the help of your circle, and by tapping into your resilient nature, victory is always achieved.

WAIT 5 SECONDS

Now that the image of the dark being has been transmuted to helpful energy, move it to the left of you. The newly calibrated energy beam now constantly reminds you that you are more powerful than any problem in your life. You hold all the keys to your own victory, you are the one with all the power.

Now once more begin to visualize in front of you a new image. This image is very different, it holds no real dimension nor any real structure. This entity floating effortlessly in front of you is change itself. You notice that the color of this image is pure green, vibrantly changing constantly its size and shape. It begins to emit a beam of light with the same green tint to it. This time the ray moves into your stomach and begins to instruct you that change is to be welcomed, that is a natural occurrence such as time and space. It begins to teach you that you have the ability to change anything about yourself and to deal with any change in your life naturally. The more you understand that change is a constant and beneficial factor in your life and those around you, the more you obtain the ability to change yourself. This power that this entity is sending you allows you to adapt to any situation effortlessly, making you even more powerful and resourceful than before. Now look once more at your family and friends, they too are connected to this change, they too are adapting to every situation. You realize you are not alone, and that any and all change can be dealt with in a positive way. Allow this being to fill you with the power to be able to adapt to anything in your life. You are the agent of change, you are the one that molds yourself to fit any situation and once you calibrate your own being to fit the change, it ceases to feel like adversity and becomes a powerful tool in your life. Realize that change is what sets you free from your current situation, and that you should welcome change in your life at all times. You are the supreme master of change, and there is no situation in your life you cannot overcome.

WAIT 5 SECONDS

Move this being of change behind you, now that you have become its master, change follows you wherever you go, whatever action you take. Now change doesn't govern your life, but instead allows you to use it to propel you into a greater tomorrow. All three beams of light makes you more resilient and effective in your life, in all ways.

Once more begin to picture in front of you a new image. This being is a bright red color and vibrates like the sun. It's energy is incredibly quick and powerful. As it sends you its ray of energy it moves that energy right into the front of your mind. The moment your body makes contact with the light energy you understand exactly what it is; decisive actions. This is all of your actions, your decisions. It is quick and to the point and always allows you to make the best decisions in any situation. The red vibrant ray begins to open your perception to easily see the big picture behind what is happening in your life. With this ally in your life you know that you will be able to make the right choices to make any problem dissolve. It is mighty and powerful and is even with all of its strength, it is still only a part of who you are. Feel how this force is giving you the ability to understand and overcome all obstacles and challenges in your life. Anchor the power of this light deep into the frontal cortex of your brain, it is activated whenever you are presented with a problem and will give you easy access to all the positive and creative solutions to deal with any problem. Allow it to recalibrate your mind right now.

WAIT 5 SECONDS

As the power of this light peaks inside of your mind, move the image right above you. Allow it to float above your head like a beacon of light, guiding you through the darkness. This will always be working all the time, it will provide you with the essential decision making power to make quick work of any challenge.

Take one second and look at all the elements around you; your friends and family, the change behind you, the vibrant decision making powers above you, and the transmuted power of challenges in your life, bowing down to you. Feel how all of these rays coming from these elements make you stronger and more successful, a winner in any and all situations.

Now in front of you begin to visualize a new image. This element has a pure yellow color to it, vibrating with passion, energy, and vigor. This being represents your steps towards obtaining your goals. No matter what occurs in your life, you will always be moving towards your goals, this energy will always pull you in the right direction based on the decisions you make to solve any and all problems in your life. Feel how the yellow ray hits your feet, making them feel warm and full of energy. The more the ray of light bathes your feet the more impulse you have towards completing your next goals. The energy is telling you that by moving forward, even through the most challenging situation, you will always walk out unharmed and better. Allow this energy to motivate you to your next goals right now.

Take this element now and move it further into the distance in front of you and elevate it like a beacon of light, guiding you to your next goal. You can feel the pull from it as you move it, motivating you to keep on going at all times. Take a moment to feel the pull and notice how the element of "decisive actions" hovering above your head and this yellow energy of "moving towards your goals" are connected. They both work in perfect harmony allowing you to always see the solution and to always move to the next goal you have on your path to victory and success.

WAIT 5 SECONDS

Now once more in front of you begin to picture a new element. This one has a bright white color, radiating like the sun. It has a warm and very peaceful feel to it. This white element is "self discovery" and is a constant occurrence in your life. Instead of a beam of light coming from it towards you, the entire energy surrounds you as if it was your aura. It works as a protective shield against any and all adverse moments in your life, reminding you that no matter how difficult a situation might seem, everything occurs to teach you more of who you are. As this energy vibrates around you, begin to understand that self-discovery is a constant factor in your life and any and all elements around you are simply helping you discover the greatness of who you are. This energy is a fundamental part of who you are, and whispers in your ear the secrets of _you_ whenever you are confronted by any situation. Allow this energy to anchor itself all around you and to become an active part of your daily life.

WAIT 5 SECONDS

The next element that appears in front of you has a warm orange color to it, this vibrating energy is known as perspective. As it fully appears in front of you it begins to send a warm vibrating ray of light directly to your eyes. As it touches both eyes you suddenly begin to have an eagle eye perspective of your life. You realize that there is always more to life than meets the eye and that no matter what situation you are confronted with, you can perceive all good things in your life, all the time. This energy protects you from falling into the trap of narrow perception and rather allows you to become objective within your life. Feel how your eyes are changing due to this light energy. You can now see things much more clearly and can see the truth about your own life easily and effortlessly. Your perception will, from this moment on, always see the big picture. The more the ray of light touches your eyes, the more you begin to absorb this energy into your eyes. This energy is becoming your eyes and will always be with you in every waking moment of your life allowing you to see more than what is happening right in front of you. Take some time and anchor this energy deep into your eyes, fuse it together with your body, spirit and mind.

WAIT 5 SECONDS

As this element completely becomes part of your body, mind and soul, you can now see that your eyes are vibrating the same warm orange color as the element. This means that it has become an integral part of who you are.

Another element begins to form in front of you, this one holding a light blue energy. This energy is called "hope" and will always keep your chin up even through adversity. As this hopeful energy becomes bigger and manifests itself in your space, it sends its ray of light directly to your heart. As it touches your heart you can feel how hope flows effortlessly in your life. No matter what the situation, no matter what the problem, you always maintain a hopeful outlook on it and can easily find the right solution. Hope now is becoming a part of your life, it will always be there with you and will keep you even when you find yourself in a dark situation. See how this element of hope enters your heart and becomes a physical part of it. Your heart begins to shine with this light blue energy, signifying that hope is becoming a natural part of your life and will always be with you no matter what. Allow this energy to anchor itself deep inside you and see how your heart and your eyes now are connected. Your perception will always guide you to hopeful solutions. This is your nature now, this is who you are.

WAIT 5 SECONDS

Finally begin to notice a new element appear. This element has a peach color to it. Unlike the rest, the energy isn't vibrant but rather smooth and peaceful. This peach colored energy represents how you take care of yourself. As it manifests in your space, feel its energy surround you, feel the love it has for you. It takes care of your body, mind and health and motivates you to eat better, do more exercise and to generally maintain a positive attitude in your life regardless of any situation. This energy sends you a peach colored peaceful beam and as it touches you, you instantly feel the need to maintain your body, mind and spirit in optimal conditions. In fact, this energy is so strong that taking care of yourself is something you enjoy. You love to be healthy, you love to be strong and intelligent, you love to be feeling good and thus from this moment on you will always do what is best for your body and mind. This energy remains static right in front of you, it is what you always look out for, and the filter through which you see yourself and your world. You know that your body is a perfect machine able to do anything, as well as your mind, able to see far beyond time and space itself.

Anchor this energy, this feeling deep inside you and realize that it is a fundamental part of who you are. Allow it to seep in and form a part of you.

WAIT 5 SECONDS

Take one moment and notice all the elements around and inside you, this circle of excellence is what keeps you stable during any situation, it is your network of resilience. With these elements around you, you will always know how to land on your feet, you will always be able to bounce back from any situation. This network of power can never be removed unless you command it; you have created the perfect internal and external force to guide you effortlessly through any challenge in life. They all work together to make you the best version of you. This is your network of strength, power, and resilience and these elements are your allies. Allow this circle to form a fundamental part of who you are.

As the feeling of power and creative perception rises, clench your fists together and anchor the feeling.

(Allow client to hold anchor for 30 seconds and release)

Whenever you feel that you don't know what to do, simply clench your fists again to come back to this place, it is the method to reach your circle of excellence in no time.

Take some time now in silence and allow your mind to integrate, for your best and highest good, the beneficial suggestions you have just received.

(Exit trance in your preferred manner.)

Master of All Decisions

About the script

This script is useful for the client who needs to make stronger decisions in their life; decisions that will lead to more desirable outcomes. It is useful in helping people to break patterns in their decision making behavior. Prior to this session, it is helpful for the client to do some pre-work around the ecology of their decisions, or to have pre-session dialogue about this.

Review what the client feels that they want in their life, and have them ask themselves the following questions:

If I could have it now, would I take it?
Are all costs and consequences of achieving your outcome, including the time involved, acceptable to you and anyone else affected by it?

This is known as ecology. Consider the costs, consequences, environmental and third party impact of having the outcome. This can be done in a dialogue but is an excellent written or journaling exercise that can be done over the course of several days prior to a session.

If at any point during the course of this session, the client runs up against an internal disagreement with that step in the process, the client should be emerged from trance and the issue discussed. Perhaps more homework, journaling or discussing the desired outcome with others, will be required or perhaps the client may realize that they hadn't weighed all the costs involved in their desired outcome and may alter their goals. This should all be viewed as beneficial and part of the process of conscious life creation. What holds people back or creates self sabotage in their lives is most often not having walked through this process thoroughly and completely, and an unresolved question in their subconscious mind exists that is a barrier to achieving what they believe they desire.

While this session can be delivered in a recording with the proper amount of coaching beforehand, it is truly best done one on one with a client, obtaining ideomotor responses to the completion of each section and giving you the ability to emerge the client and discuss any internal disagreement that may arise.

Script: *Master of All Decisions*

USE YOUR PREFERRED INDUCTION METHOD

As you sit here in this relaxed position, completely and fully focused on these words we will begin to take a journey. Throughout this journey you will obtain and embed the essential skills of making superb and beneficial decisions. Once you have learned this technique it will be forever part of your core structure and will automatically spring into action whenever you are faced with any decision in your life.

For now, simply think of an important decision that you need to make in your life at this moment. Make sure that the decision you must make holds value in your life. As you think about the decision, the first question you will ask yourself in a loud audible voice within your mind is; "What do I want to create?"

"What do I want to create." Define exactly what you want in positive present terms. Imagine the most successful outcome you can. See what day it is when you achieve the positive outcome of your decision, the exact time when you knew that you had made it. Always ask the question in the positive, only in the positive. If you want something to go away or something to stop from happening, then simply say the opposite of what it is you want to achieve. For instance if you say; "I want to stop fighting" you can say "I want peace" and so on. Take a few moments and really dissect your desire, know exactly what it is you want and formulate one solid sentence in your mind about what it is you want. Start the sentence with "I am creating" and complete it with your desire or need.

(Wait 15 seconds or ask client for ideomotor response to indicate when they've formulated their outcome.)

Good! Now that you have dissected your desires, you know exactly what it is you want. This is the first step in making an effective decision that will lead to the actions that will achieve your desires. With this first step you are activating your Reticular Activating System. The Reticular Activating System is the area in your brain that focuses your conscious mind on the most important information that your subconscious observes every single minute of the day. It is your mental filter and will continually be searching for a way to achieve your needs and desires. It is the filter to all your perception and now is beginning to focus on obtaining the outcome of your decision.

Now that your Reticular Activating System has been activated, you will intensify it. Repeat one more time "What it is you want to create" in your mind. Now ask yourself: "Is it Achievable?"

Think long and hard on whether this decision is physically achievable. See in your mind's eye how you are achieving it, what you need to achieve it and what you need to do. Has this already been done by someone else? See and imagine how that person achieved it. When you envision yourself achieving your goal, see how easily you are doing it, effortlessly. See how everything is falling in the right place, see how all your effort paid off brilliantly. Envision exactly how you are achieving your desired outcome. Take a few seconds to imagine your achievement.

(Wait 5 seconds)

Now in your mind simply state "It is achievable and I can achieve it" while thinking about your desire. Say it as loud as you can in your mind, scream it, proclaim it to the world. As you say "It is Achievable and I can achieve it" envision how you are achieving it, how you are the master of all your decisions.

(Wait 3 seconds)

Excellent!

Now that you know "What it is you want to create" and that you can achieve it, your Reticular Activating System is even more in tune with your desires. You have increased the intensity of its function and it is working on obtaining your desired outcome even as you relax there, bringing you closer to your goal every passing second.

Simply relax and allow it to do its work. Now it is time to create the criteria of your successful outcome, the evidence to your victory. Just ask yourself; "What physical evidence will prove to me and others that I have achieved my desired outcome?"

Is this evidence something you can see, touch, smell, hear or taste? Is it something that you can show other people? How can you prove that you have truly obtained your desired outcome? Think about this for a moment, think about specific things that will help you demonstrate the success of your desired outcome.

(Wait 5 seconds, or ask client for ideomotor response.)

Perfect! Now that you know "What it is you want to create" and that you can achieve it and also demonstrate to yourself and others, your Reticular Activating System has increased the intensity of its function even more. It is actively looking for each and every solution, measuring each and every decision and action, to bring you closer to your desired outcome. You will begin to notice opportunities; you will notice your brain working every single passing second on making your desires come true. Rest in the FACT that your mind is now on your side, it is your ally and will do whatever it can to bring you closer to success.

Now; take a moment to think about whether this decision is under your control. Do you hold the keys to making it happen? Make sure that the decision is yours to make, that you are the master of your own decisions in this area of your life. Always focus on things that you can control, authorize or arrange. It must be within your grasp to obtain it. Meditate for a few moments on whether the decision is truly in your power.

(Wait 3 seconds)

Good! Now that you know "What it is you want to create" and that you can achieve it and have the evidence to prove your success. You also know that this decision is completely in your power, it's under your control. Your Reticular Activating System is now beginning to work on hyper drive, it is finding absolutely all necessary connections to allow you to make clear and concise, accurate decisions. Your brain is actively working on making your desires come true.

Now, begin to think about the costs involved in obtaining your desired outcome. Think about what it is you need to do to make it happen. The time you need to invest, the effort and sacrifice that is required to obtain your outcome. Think about the consequences to your decision, what impact it would have on the environment or any third parties. Take a few moments to really dissect the costs or impacts involved and make peace with it. Accept the consequences if it doesn't impact negatively on anyone, yourself included. Take these moments to think about it.

(Wait 5 seconds, or ask client for ideomotor response.)

Excellent! Now you know "What it is you want to create" and that you can achieve it and that you have the evidence to prove your successful outcome. You know that this decision is in your power and have accepted all costs or impacts involved in obtaining your desired outcome; your Reticular Activating System is fine tuning itself to deliver optimal results. It is only speeding up the process and becoming even more effective.

Now, begin to think about what resources you require to obtain your desired outcome. What do you need to have to make it happen? What special knowledge do you possess to speed up the process? How can your belief system help you achieve your desired outcome? What physical objects do you have to bring you closer? Who do you know that can assist you with this decision? How much money do you need to have to make this happen? What's the timeframe; is time on your side or against you? What internal resources will help you the most-- decisiveness, resilience, creativity, strength, willpower, more? Think for a few moments on all of these elements, think about what it is you need to make your outcome happen.

(Wait 10 seconds, or ask client for ideomotor response)

Perfect! Now you know "What it is you want to create" and that you can achieve it, and that you have the evidence to prove the success of your outcome. Now you know that the outcome is completely in your hands and under your control and have accepted all costs and consequences to your actions and know exactly what you need to achieve your goal, your Reticular Activating System is thin slicing all the information in your brain, bringing you closer to your desired outcome at this very precise moment in time. It is working on overdrive!

Finally, begin to think about if you could have the desired outcome right now, in this very instance…would you take it? Is the time and effort involved accepted by you and those around you? Are you okay with what this desired outcome would mean for other people and yourself? If this outcome was right here in front of you right now, would you hesitate or take it in this moment? Truly search your heart and mind and make sure that you are ready to make this commitment right now. Take these moments to search deep inside your mind and heart.

(Wait 5 seconds, or ask client for ideomotor response)

Perfect! Now you know exactly "What it is you want to create" and that you CAN achieve it and have all the evidence to prove that you have achieved your outcome. Now that you know that you control the outcome of your decision and have accepted all costs and consequences of your actions and have weighed out the impact on yourself, other people and the environment. Now that you have accepted the fact that you can make this decision right now, and be perfectly fine and at peace with the decision, you have completely and utterly engaged your Reticular Activating System. Right now your brain is sifting through all the information presented, it is focused on providing the best possible solution. It will continue to do so throughout the rest of your life, with any decision you make, any creation you undertake. Simply remember the process and you can intensify your Reticular Activating system to provide more thorough solutions, clearer timelines and solid decisions.

Right now you are ready to make the decision and begin taking action, you have weighed out the consequences and analyzed every bit of information involved. This is the best decision you can make, it brings you closer to your desired outcome. Your body will respond in accordance to your mind's decisions and you will automatically have the desire to take the right actions to making it happen. You are ready now!

USE PREFERRED METHOD TO BREAK TRANCE

No Failure, Just Feedback - The Selective Membrane

About the Script

One of my favorite tenets of Neurolinguistic Programming is the concept that there is no such thing as failure, only feedback. If you use the results you've gotten in the past as a learning tool, change and adjust your behaviors to get different results and view the past as a school from which to learn, you will be much more successful (and more resilient) than those who entertain feelings of guilt and remorse beyond their usefulness.

This script was written to install this as a belief, as a working filter for your efforts and results, and to create an attitude of continuous improvement for your future.

Script: No Failure, Just Feedback - The Selective Membrane

USE YOUR PREFERRED INDUCTION METHOD

Imagine that you are floating in a huge white space. There are absolutely no limitations within this space; you have absolute control over every single element within this space in time. This is the center of your being; this is the place where all thought processes, conscious and unconscious occur. Here you have absolute control over every thought, emotion, dream, strength, belief, or fear you may have within your life. This is also the place where you can change anything of yourself and it will have a permanent, lasting effect in your life. Take a moment to breathe in the power and authority you have here. Take a moment to feel your surroundings and to understand your power. Look at yourself as a being of amazing power, of absolute control. Here you are the master of your own being, of your own decisions and all your collective life experience. You have the ability to travel into your own past, explore your present and define your future. Take this moment to understand that you are in complete control.

(WAIT FIVE SECONDS)

Now we will begin to open a door in your past. It's very easy to do. Simply imagine a door with a door handle. See how it appears right in front of you by simply imagining it. Look how big it is, look how strong it is and how firm it is. Inside your hand you have a master key that can open any door within your soul, it allows you access to any part of your brain. Take the key and insert it into the keyhole and turn it to the right. Listen how the lock clicks signifying that the door is now unlocked. Press on the door and open it completely. You can feel a cool wind coming from the opened door; these are all your memories and past thoughts and experiences blowing on you. Whatever your mind focuses on now will allow any past memory to come through that door. You can select which past experience, which past memory comes through that door by merely thinking about it.

For now you will only focus on all the moments where you have succeeded in the past. Think about every single victory, every single wonderful achievement, and every single moment that you felt like an absolute champion. See how these memories come out in the form of pure white streams of light. Notice how it begins to fill the room with these wonderful memories where you were victorious in the past. Think about every prize you have won, every obstacle you have overcome, every single achievement you have gained. The more you think about it the brighter and more powerful these white streaks of light are becoming. For the next ten seconds, simply magnify the strength of these streaks of light. Allow the memories to become vivid and alive.

(WAIT TEN SECONDS)

Now that these memories have peaked and that you can see the vibrancy and power surrounding them, cup your hands together. As you cup your hands together you notice that all of these wonderful victorious thoughts travel towards your cupped hand. The more of these streaks that enter your cupped hand the brighter it shines. These streaks of light become so dense that it forms a pure white glowing liquid in the palms of your hands. See how the liquid fills up to the brim of your cupped hands with this wonderful and cool liquid of success. This liquid is the condensed version of all your past experiences of success, every single time you have done something brilliant. It is absolutely every single victory you have achieved in the past. Feel the cool texture of the liquid in the palms of your hands, feel the vibrant energy and happiness that surround this liquid. Look into the silvery essence of the liquid and realize that this is you in every single way shape and form.

Put your lips to it and take a small sip of the liquid, feel how it travels down your throat and into your body. Feel how the liquid pulsates through your veins, refreshing your vigor and strength, multiplying your confidence. This is your absolute success; this is every victory you have acquired throughout your life. The vibrant energy of the liquid tickles your hands; it is so pure and perfect.

With this liquid still cupped in your hands, lift it as high as you can above your head. Not a single drop is spilled; it is perfectly in place as you control every single element within your being. As you have the liquid cupped above your head, simply move your hands to your sides once more leaving the liquid above your head. Notice that as you let go of the liquid it remains in place as a silver orb of bright liquid hovering above your head. You can feel the vibrant energy emitting from the hovering liquid orb.

Now, focus on that floating orb and multiply its power. Make it stronger, feel how every minute you focus on that orb, the energy becomes increasingly stronger. The energy vibrates even into your bones, the frequency changing your interior, imprinting success and confidence deep into your tiniest cell. As this feeling begins to peak, notice how the orb is beginning to surround you like a bubble. As it grows it first surrounds your head, changing your vision of the world outside. As you look through this bubble from the inside looking out, you can see only victory and you can see only success in everything you will do.

As the bubble begins to grow it expands to the point of now covering both your head and your chest. The bubble is now almost half way around your body. You can feel that your heart and internal organs are beaming with success and victory. Each and every internal organ is now functioning in a paradigm of pure success. They are stronger than any challenge, physical, mental, emotional, from within or without, and will supply you with the necessary energy to achieve victory as they now work perfectly together.

Notice the bubble now grow even more and covering you from your head to your knees. You can feel that your upper thighs and knees feel strong and powerful. They can take you to your victory and you will always be able to reach your goals. Now the bubble finally grows to completely cover you from head to toes. You are now standing inside of the bubble that once was a liquid orb of pure success. This bubble acts as a selective membrane, only allowing in what is good and filtering out everything that harms your perception and mind. This selective membrane is composed of all your victories, all your success, all your determination in the world. It allows you to see through all lies, hurtful comments and critiques and shows you the real truth behind it.

As you breathe now, feel the air inside of the bubble fill your lungs. Feel the energy vibrating from within this protective bubble of success. Allow the feeling to peak to new levels and strengthen the bubble even more.

(WAIT FIVE SECONDS)

Now face the door again but this time think of all past failures, past mistakes and errors you may have made. As you think about these things notice a fowl black streak of light come from the door opening. This is every single bad thought, failure and mistake you have made in the past. This is your tainted past, everything that you are ashamed of, everything that makes you doubt yourself, every negative comment, every embarrassing moment you have experienced.

Notice how fowl the smell is. As these feelings and past experiences come through the door you notice that it automatically wishes to go to your heart and mind. The purpose of these black streaks of light is to convince you that you are not good enough, that you are a failure. Normally these thoughts would affect you significantly, but now that you have a bubble of victory acting as a selective membrane you notice that the black streaks of light, right as it touches the white gleaming bubble, filters out the darkness. As it passes through the selective membrane you notice that all of the black dark light simply falls to the floor and disappears. The only thing that is allowed to enter through the selective membrane is the truth hidden within these past negative experiences. What comes through the bubble is only the feedback on how you have tried. What you have learned and how this perceived negative experience was nothing more than a step in your development. It is what made you the person you are today and taught you the necessary skills to be a success.

The selective membrane instructs you that every bad experience was merely a lesson you had to learn. Every negative memory that travels through this selective membrane now reveals just how brave you were for even attempting it and that even though you may have thought it to be a failure, turned out to be the necessary steps to achieving victory.

Notice how each and every single past negative experience travels through the door and into the bubble. It is filtering absolutely every negative thought and turning it into positive feedback, revealing to you the necessary truths to be a success every single second of your day. Allow all your negative thoughts, past experiences and failures to travel through the door. Allow your bubble of success to change the core structure of all negative experience and convert it into positive feedback. Empty yourself from all negative experiences right now.

(WAIT FIVE SECONDS OR ASK FOR IDEOMOTOR RESPONSE)

Now that you have managed to pour out all negative past experiences, notice that the bubble only became stronger. Every single time a negative experience occurs or a major decision needs to be taken, the bubble is activated. It is with you all day and will from this moment on continually filter out all bad experiences, all negative comments and only show you the truth, the success behind each thought.

Right now close the door once more and lock it. You have now managed to place a selective membrane around you that will always protect you from any negative comment or situation; it will always keep your mind focused on achieving success and victory. It has replaced all notions of failure and has implemented a powerful paradigm of success. This bubble is indestructible and will guide you for the rest of your life. This is a permanent membrane that from this moment on will always dictate accurate and helpful feedback, regardless of the situation.

Once more realize that you have absolute power in this space, and the things you do here have a lasting effect on your life. This membrane is now as much a part of you as your hands and feet, your mind and heart. It is you and guides your perception to only and always focus on the good and positive. From this moment on you will continue to walk towards your own victory and success, every single waking and sleeping second of your life. You now are completely free from all past mistakes; you can now see them for what they really are. Steps towards your ultimate success.

Take some time now in silence and allow your mind to integrate, for your best and highest good, the beneficial suggestions you have just received.

(Exit trance in your preferred manner.)

Totem of Power and Confidence

About the Script

This script also combines hypnosis and principles from Neurolinguistic Programming. People tend to respond very powerfully to this script. It is appropriate for people who have a difficult time connecting to their own sense of personal power, of being "at cause" in their lives. Use it as part of a process of ego strengthening and creating a sense of personal power. This script performs well when used in conjunction with "Master of All Decisions" and "No Failure, Only Feedback."

*NOTE: Prior to the hypnosis session, ask that your client bring a small object of great importance with him/her. When you begin let them hold this object (totem) in their right hand. Start induction process.

Script: Totem of Power and Confidence

USE YOUR PREFERRED INDUCTION METHOD

Pay VERY close attention to my voice as you enter into a deep relaxed state of mind. You are in a place where everything is possible, where you are in control of your emotions and your decisions. Your body responds completely to what ever command you may utter, you are in charge and have all the power right in the palm of your hand.

SEE in your mind's eye a big tall beautiful room, with a pure white light radiating all around you. This room is YOUR room, it is the place where everything is possible. This room sits in the middle of your mind, it is YOUR command post where you can speak directly to your EMOTIONS, your THOUGHTS, your CREATIVITY, your PEACE, your STRENGTH, your BODY and absolutely every single aspect of your life. It is in this room where you make the decisions of VICTORY in YOUR life, this is your SOURCE of confidence and only YOU have access to it. You can enter the room whenever you want, during every single waking moment of your life, you alone hold the keys to THIS room. SEE it (wait 5 seconds) See the walls, and how they comfort you, FEEL the floor of the room and how the warmth relaxes you, BREATHE the air and feel it fill your lungs with POWER and

CONFIDENCE. HEAR the calm soothing quietness YOU have created deep inside you. As you LOOK, TOUCH, FEEL and BREATHE the air you notice the white light around you become STRONGER until it fills your entire body from head to toe.

FEEL how the white light touches your feet, and how it becomes as light as AIR. Now FEEL it slowly climb up to your calves and relax your muscles completely. NOW feel it climb up to your thighs, the stress and worry simply melts off. It slowly climbs up and touches your hips, it frees it COMPLETELY and you can EASILY move as YOU wish. Now it is in your stomach, radiating a warm confident feeling deep in your belly. The light now is in your chest. As your chest expands and you breathe in you FEEL it relax completely. It climbs up to your neck, all the tension and all the stress and all the worry EVAPORATES and leaves your body. It is replaced with a RELAXED and CONFIDENT feeling, injecting POWER into your body. YOU are free to move as you please, you are in control. Finally the warm white light moves up to your head. IT consumes you completely. Your head becomes LIGHT, it becomes FREE. The white light allows you to control your thinking, your EMOTIONS, your decisions, your state of confidence. The light now is a part of you. It is over you, on top of you, inside your lungs, your heart, your kidneys, your stomach, in your veins. You and the white warm radiating light are the same thing. You and the room are the same thing. You feel and control everything in your CONTROL room, where YOU have the power. Take a few moments to absorb the room and everything in it. Realize that this room is only an extension of yourself, it is your THRONE of POWER. You have the POWER to bring into this room anything you want, and you have the power to exclude anything you want. You are the master as well as the gatekeeper. YOU are in control every single second you are in your POWER room.

Now…Imagine there is a door on the far side of the room opposite to you. It is a magnificent door with beautiful decorations. It is the most beautiful door you have ever seen. The door makes you feel warm and good about yourself since you are the only one who can open it and close it. You have ALL the control, you have ALL the authority, you are (King/Queen) of this place.

Walk over to the door and reach out and grab the handle. As you touch the handle feel good thoughts and vibrations radiating from it. Feel it combine with the white light that is inside you and all around you. AS you open the door slowly, you peek through it. On the other side you see all the thoughts, experiences and dreams you have ever had. This is the place where your ideas are born, it is a magical place where anything is possible at YOUR command. As you stare out into this wonderful space of thought and dream, command YOUR best experiences to come to you.

EVERY SINGLE good experience is rushing to you right now. EVERY experience that makes you feel STRONG, CONFIDENT, POWERFUL, HAPPY, IN CHARGE, WORTHY, LOVED, CARED FOR, WONDERFUL, REFRESHED, INSPIRED, RELAXED, AMAZING. Take two minutes to think of all the past experiences and future experiences that make you feel like this, and bring them to you… into your room of POWER and CONFIDENCE. As they come in they become part of the room, decorating it with everything you LOVE and CHERISH.

As these experiences, and feelings enter your ROOM of POWER and CONFIDENCE, notice that each experience connects itself with everything in the room. EVERY single aspect of the room is connected to you, as you and room are one. As these experiences accommodates themselves in the room in the perfect arrangement, close the door behind you and walk to the center of the room.

As you stand in the center of the room begin to imagine a throne right in front of you. This is YOUR throne, your seat of authority where you control ALL aspects of your being. Look at how majestic it is, as it reflects absolutely everything good you have ever done and will ever do. It is the perfect continuous action o excellence that you possess; it is your seat of POWER. See how the warm and calm white light is especially powerful all around your throne. Notice how all the good and powerful experiences channel themselves to the throne, making it glow with power and excellence.

Slowly climb up to the throne and take your seat. This is your rightful place, where you are master and (King/Queen). Your wish is the command of your body, mind and spirit. Every aspect of your life obeys you completely while in this room of POWER and CONFIDENCE, while sitting on your THRONE. Take a moment to feel all the authority and power you possess. Only goodness and excellence surrounds you now, YOU CAN DO ANYTHING YOU WISH.

IMAGINE in your RIGHT hand a scepter. It is beautiful and adorned with jewels. Each Jewel represents the good experiences of Confidence and power, of excellence and joy you brought into the room. SEE how each jewel reflects the essence of what is in that room. This SCEPTER represents all your power and confidence you have. IT represents your room of POWER and CONFIDENCE, everything you have achieved and will ever achieve is in this SCEPTER. IT is your mobile room of POWER and CONFIDENCE.

Wherever you go and where ever you are, this SCEPTER will give you instant access into your room of power. As you hold the scepter in your right hand, focus all your energy, everything you are feeling in this precise moment, every victory, every good feeling, every powerful feeling, every warm feeling, every joyful experience into the SCEPTER. SEE how the jewels begin to shine and radiate the warm and POWERFUL light. IT becomes impregnated with everything in the room. IT is FULL of POWER and CONFIDENCE and it is subject only to you.

With this scepter in your hand, you can feel the authority pulse throughout your body, you can feel the incredible power radiate in your hands. Focus on these feelings and as it reaches its climax, squeeze the scepter in your hands.

This scepter is your totem of POWER and CONFIDENCE. It is the object you brought with you today. As the feelings of overwhelming confidence and power reaches its climax, squeeze the object and realize that the scepter and the object in your right hand is the same. Every time you need to access your ROOM of POWER and CONFIDENCE, you only have to squeeze your TOTEM of POWER and CONFIDENCE once, and you will be instantly transported back to your THRONE of POWER and CONFIDENCE. Where you are (KING/QUEEN) alone, master of your emotions, and your decisions. Feel how the TOTEM begins to radiate with the same white light that surrounds you, that is inside of you and all over your room. Squeeze it one more time and seal it in. YOUR TOTEM of POWER and CONFIDENCE.

Now as I count back from five you will become more aware of your surroundings.

5 – You begin to wake up and become aware of your surroundings

4 – You feel refreshed and relaxed

3 – You are more awake, and the feeling of POWER of CONFIDENCE is still heavy on you

2 – Your almost completely awake, you feel your TOTEM still glowing with POWER and CONFIDENCE

1 – Your waking up and back in the room, still holding the same feeling in your TOTEM

0 – You are awake, refreshed and here with me in the room.

Fuel Your Fire

About the script

This script brings together the concepts of being at cause, no failure only feedback, personal resilience and personal strength and confidence. It is a more masculine script, and may be modified as you see fit to suit your client's personality; however, I would encourage erring on the side of more authoritative rather than less and see how your client responds.

Script: Fuel Your Fire

USE PREFERRED INDUCTION METHOD

Now that you have reached a perfect moment of calmness and serenity you feel at peace. You are aware that you are in complete control of this environment; whatever you imagine can come true in this place where you rule supreme. Take a moment to fill your presence to the furthest corner of this room, claim your dominance over this space. Nothing can stand in your way; nothing can deny you of your desires in this place.

In this place, where you are floating effortlessly in this comforting space, you have the ability to call forth any problem and demand a solution and it will come, you can remember any memory and create any vision as you choose. You have absolute control over everything that occurs within this space. Make this become a reality, accept this to be true right now.

WAIT 5 SECONDS

Right now begin to think about your life. Think about the problems you are currently facing, the issues that are holding you back from achieving what it truly is you want in life. As you think on these problems that are popping in your mind as I speak begin to manifest them in your space. Externalize the problems and the issues, see them outside of yourself, in this space where you have complete control.

Notice that these problems, these issues have to obey you in this room, in this space where you are master of all. Notice as these problems and issues manifest how weak they truly are compared to you. Where you float like a god/dess in this space of power these problems shrivel in your presence. Notice that once you externalized the problem and looked at it that it no longer has any power over you.

Look at your problems now, how small and dismal they really are compared to you. These problems no longer have any power over you. No longer do you feel unworthy, no longer do you feel weak or intimidated. You are the supreme ruler of this space, of your body and your mind.

Allow your authority to grow and realize that you can command these problems to do anything you desire. They can disappear, be melted to nothing or solved. You have to only choose and they must obey. You are the master here.

WAIT 5 SECONDS

Now command these problems to be solved and disappear and replace them with strength and understanding. Realize that these problems weren't problems, these issues holding you back weren't issues but rather opportunity. These are moments you face to teach yourself about your own strengths and abilities. It challenges you to become better and stronger. Now you know that you are the one who commands the outcomes and that these issues are merely lessons.

Know that every step you take echoes into history. Your life matters and you impact people on a daily basis. You help people, you make others become better versions of themselves, similar as you are continually bettering yourself.

Feel confidence and power enter through your nostrils. Feel strength and perseverance pump through your veins. Every breath empowers you more, it fuels your sense of purpose.

WAIT 10 SECONDS

There is nothing you cannot do if you put your mind to it. There is no failure there is only victory. Every unsuccessful attempt is bringing you one step closer to success. Every success launches you to greater successes. You are powerful, you are smart. You are inspiring and charismatic.

Realize right now that you have the ability to make every dream come true, you have the ability to inspire that in others. There is no defeat, there is only success!

In this moment take this feeling of victory and squeeze your hands in the form of a fist. Press this power deep into your hands and realize that when you come out of this space you will take the authority and victory with you. When you clench your hands in victory you will become the same powerhouse you are in this space because there is no difference for your mind here or in your waking life.

Take this moment to clench hard and to bring this power deep into your core right now.

WAIT 10 SECONDS

When you come out of this session, when you are fully aware of everything that is around you; you will be in complete control of your life, vigor and strength course through your veins. Your heart pumps with Fire Fueled by your strength and powerful insight on life. You are on the right path and you are success itself.

USE PREFERRED METHOD TO BREAK TRANCE

Part 2: Scripts for Weight Release and Healthier Habits

Eliminate Sugar

About the script

I wrote this script after reading the book, Salt, Sugar, Fat: How the Food Giants Hooked Us by Michael Moss. There's no argument that sugar is addictive; that made the news in 2013 as an "official' fact, based on research. The idea that we should need to be told this is silly, of course. If you look at the increase in the amount of sugar eaten per capita between 1800 and today, and the concomitant increase in obesity and diabetes, the connection is obvious. What angered me, and prompted this script, was that the addictive properties of sugar, salt and fat have been intentionally used to hook us on processed foods in the name of profit.

One of the ways the subconscious mind learns is through heightened emotion. This script would be best used after a discussion of what's been going on in the processed food industry, how we've been used as unwitting guinea pigs for the profit of Big Food, and ideally after your client reads the Moss book, or another like it. Use the feelings of anger, betrayal and indignation to create fertile ground in the mind for positive change!

Script: Eliminate Sugar

Sit or lie back in a comfortable position, close your eyes if you haven't already done so. Take a deep breath in and just feel your body relaxing with that exhale. Let it all go with your breathe. Let thoughts go, concerns, expectations, worries of the day, let it all leave you with that outward breath. As you continue to take a series of deep relaxing breaths, feel yourself letting go. Because this is time for you. Time to relax and focus on yourself. On what is going to improve your life, your experience, mentally, physically, emotionally and in all ways. Focusing on yourself. Because you deserve to focus on yourself. And this is the time for you. Sacred time. With every breath feel your body relaxing a little bit more and more. Because the breath is a natural relaxer for the body. And as the body relaxes the mind slows down. And as the mind slows down the body relaxes even more completely. Like a carousel that's come to the end of the ride, picture it spinning more slowly with every turn, slower, gently coming to a stop, coming to rest. As you allow every process and function in your body and mind to come to a rest right now. That's right. Feel how much more relaxed you are right now than you were just a minute ago. And you may wonder to yourself how much more relaxed you can become. And as I count backwards from five down to zero you can allow, imagine or just even pretend that every number from five down to zero represents a deeper level of this relaxation. A more profound state of rest for both your body and your mind. And so let's rest more deeply now, with five, four, three, two, one, zero, zero. Zero is deep sleep. Deep sleep.

Allow that profound rest to deepen even more as you continue to listen to the sound of my voice. And I would like you to begin by reflecting on your ability to learn. It's something that we often take for granted especially as we move into the older, middle aged years or wherever we are in our lives. When we get away from being a student, where we are so focused on learning. We start to take it for granted and we might even move into a phase of our lives where we don't think that we are learning new things. But we constantly are. We are constantly learning new things. From the small to the profound and I would like you to reflect on your ability to learn now. The things that you've learned in the last week about yourself, in the last couple of weeks about food, about your abilities, about the world around you, from the small to the profound. You are learning constantly. It's the human state. We can't not learn. We are wired for learning. Look back, reflect on all of the years of experience, the times when you have intentionally learned, when you set out to learn about a new subject or topic or issue in your life and you've educated yourself about it or been educated by enrolling in a class. And the unintentional learning. Things that you learned as a result of moving through your day. The times when you said well, that worked good, I'll do that again or I won't do that again. All of that is learning. You have a powerful ability to learn. Better than any other creature known you have an amazing ability to learn and to utilize that learning, not only in the moment, but to change your course of action as you move forward in life. That is the gift of being human. That you can apply what you learned today, not only to today, but tomorrow and next week and next month and next year and next decade and on and on.

And right now you are learning about food, about how your body works, about how your mind works, about how all of these pieces interact. And one of the things I would like you to learn right now and learn really well is that sugar is addictive. They've done studies and they know that sugar lights up your brain like cocaine. And there is a very good reason for that. Way back before people had agriculture and before we refined sugar from beets or sugar cane, we simply didn't have that ability. And if you think about it, nowhere in nature does pure refined sugar exist. There is honey, and that is close, that the closest you come. But something that actually grows out of the ground, sugar cane, sugar beets, that sugar molecule is completely intertwined with other molecules. Fiber and other types of proteins and carbohydrates are combined in there. It's not an isolate. It's not pulled out just by itself. And so you could surmise based on that evidence that that's the way nature intended us to get our sugar combined with fiber and other plant proteins and other carbohydrates, not isolated, not distilled out. Because when you distill it out and make granular sugar or any of the other forms of isolated sugars that we have now it lights up the brain like a Christmas tree. It's highly addictive. Why might that be so? Because sugar has a lot of energy. And when we evolved way back before we had agriculture, your body is designed to instinctively know what foods will build up fat stores and in the past in times of human history those fat stores were important because you didn't necessarily know where your next meal was coming from. And those fat stores were important because if you caught an illness you might need that extra energy to make it through that illness. And so that's what our bodies evolved for, or designed for and that's still the state our bodies are in, because we have only been refining sugar like this for a couple hundred years. Nowhere near the time that it would take for our bodies to make genetic changes, to adapt to the kind of diet that we are giving to ourselves.

What can we learn from this? These are facts. How does facts become learning and wisdom? By putting it into action. So imagine that you, you are a human, just like a human was a hundred years ago, a thousand years ago or ten thousand years ago. Genetically just the same. Let's look at that human from ten thousand years ago. And as they hunted and they gathered, they never, almost never, ran into sugar in any sort of, anything near an isolated form, maybe they found honey. And wasn't that a rare treat? And their bodies would go Wahoo, and if they found honey they were genetically programmed to go back to that honey over and over and over and over again until it was gone. Because for survival reasons it was beneficial to put on some extra fat when you could, because there might next be a draught or a long tract to migrate to a different area, you may have just not caught game. So that's how our ancestors of ten thousand years ago interacted with sugar in their environment. Other than that, other than finding the rare source of honey, any sugar in their environment came from whole foods. It was completely wrapped up in the plant. So maybe they chewed on some sugar cane or maybe there was a beet that grew in the ground like we have sugar beets, which was particularly high in sugar content, but it was still, they ate the whole beet, so they got all the fiber, and the plant proteins, and everything else that was bound up in that beet.

In the body, then that creates a nice slow, stable blood sugar supply that's healthy. That means no diabetes, that means no incredible excess weight gain, no obesity like we have today. And so you can see these ancestors of ours roaming through their world very fit, very healthy, responding to the environment of the nature put in front of them in the way that they were designed. And remember that we are still them; genetically we are still the same. There just hasn't been enough time, even ten thousand years isn't enough time to change on an evolutionary scale the way our digestive system and blood sugar and endocrine systems work. So we are just the same as them. Look at our ancestors of one thousand years ago and their life was very much the same. There is more agriculture, but still they hadn't perfected the process of refining things. So they grew it so they could store it, so maybe they had a storehouse of wheat, but it was wheat or corn or a storehouse of apples, whole apples, or potatoes. And that's what they ate. The whole plant. And of course they had food, you know meats in their diets as well but nothing was refined.

Let's look at one hundred years ago. The refined foods began. They started to mill things more heavily, to refine wheat into enriched, the really fine bread flours and cake flours and we started to get better at it. But still people mostly ate whole foods. I remember my Dad talking about, oh my goodness, and he was born in 1930, no, I'm sorry, 1928; my Mom was born in 1930. And if they had, like they made ribbon candy for Christmas and it was just the most amazing thing, he would share these stories with me because they didn't get candy any other time of the year, candy was special, candy was rare, candy was a huge treat. Fast forward from one hundred years ago, or even less than that. 1928 almost one hundred years ago, eighty-some, and look at your mind's eye. Create a movie of the amazing changes in food refinement and production and what's available in our diets on a common everyday basis, from 1928, 1930 and when these kids were young, it was still 35, 1940, when candy was a once or twice a year treat to becoming everywhere in our diet, available every day, all the time. Now adding to the mix what we know from that book, "Salt Sugar Fat" that the heads of the big food companies, the General Mills, the Krafts, the Archer Daniels Mildlands, the Cargills, they intentionally engineered the foods to find that bliss point. The point where the food is most highly addictive. Why? Not because that's what good for us, because that's what's good for their bottom lines.

Now you have even more learning, even more knowledge. Let's turn this into wisdom, because now you can never look at sugary food the same way again. Now when you look at sugary foods you see the face of that food executive behind that sugary food and I would add that much like tobacco executives, don't smoke, food executives don't eat the junk they sell to us. They are fit and they are healthy and they don't eat the processed foods that they force onto our plates that they push at us. So every time you see a sugary food, you will now see the laughing face of a very rich, very healthy food industry executive behind it and they are laughing at you, because they think they've got you hooked. And I'm just betting that they don't. Because there is something else that you now know about sugar, the less sugar you have the less of a pull it has on you. The less sugar you have, the less you want. The less you want, the less you have. And so as you now reduce and work on perhaps even eliminating sugar from your diet, you will notice over the coming days and weeks that the less sugar you have the less sugar you will crave. And of course the less sugar you crave the less sugar you have and so you are now in charge of a healthy spiral of behavior. An upwards spiral where your life gets better and better, healthier and healthier every day. Because the less sugar you have, the less sugar you crave and the less sugar you crave the less sugar you have because you simply don't want it.

And every time you see sugar, whether it's in that basket of Easter candy or those cupcakes or the candy bars at the checkout line at the supermarket, every time you see that unhealthy food, you see a laughing food executive face behind it and they are laughing at you because they think they have you addicted. Because they have worked hard to create that bliss point, that addicted quality of their food. But you are not some robot that they can control, a puppet on strings. You are a human being with free will. And you are taking a big old pair of sheers and you are cutting those strings and setting yourself free. You are setting yourself free right now. And sticking out your tongue at that food executive and say not me. Not me. I claim my birthright to health. I claim by birthright to healthy foods and a powerful strong body. And I am not your pawn. And the less sugar I have, the less sugar I want. And the less sugar I want, the less sugar I eat. And so you are done. And I am free. And this is so. And because you have made up your mind, this is the way it is. You now decide what role sugar plays in your life. You now decide. You are not a pawn anymore. Because with knowledge comes freedom. And you are free.

Allow all of this new information, this new learning, this new wisdom and all of the changes in behavior that are going to result from this in your life starting today to become integrated into your life, into your mind and into your body in all ways and all levels now. Good. And with that learning completed and those changes in place, it is time to return to full waking consciousness as I count from one to five. Starting the count at one returning to this time and place, at two feeling positive energy flowing in from all directions, three taking a deep breath in, moving that oxygen around, four and five, eyes open wide awake feeling absolutely fantastic. Good for you.

Hypno Diet Pill

About the script

This script is a "state remembered -- state re-experienced" script, which will work best for people who have used diet pills successfully in the past, but no longer want to damage their bodies and metabolism with chemicals, or perhaps no longer have access to their preferred medication. It is one of my older scripts, and really not along the same lines as my philosophy of building up a person's resilience and ego strengthening to allow them to naturally move into healthful behaviors. However, some people may find it useful to create immediate behavioral effects that can help create weight release while continuing to work at strengthening the psyche to maintain the changes from within.

This script works along the same lines as recreating the feelings of being drunk or high with hypnosis; it is designed to create a state of hyperemperia, or "suggestion-enhanced experience."

Script: Hypno Diet Pill

USE YOUR PREFERRED INDUCTION METHOD

If you have ever taken a diet pill that really worked for you, or if you can imagine the effects that you would want to achieve from a really effective diet pill, or if you have ever had a period of time in your life where your appetite was not an issue and you only responded to your true body hunger, then you are about to embark on a journey of the mind, to experience the power of the subconscious mind to revive this experience for you, to make it real.

Simply allow your subconscious to come to the forefront of your mind now. Set your conscious mind aside. There is nothing for you to do here..now….nothing is required of you…you may simply BE. And allow your creative subconscious mind to take you on a journey…a beautiful journey that transcends time and space….a journey into the ever-present NOW… and as you set your thinking, analyzing, judging mind aside NOW, you come to a place where you can simply be….and believe. Remember when you were a little child? Yes? Remember a time, now, when you were a young child, perhaps 3, 4, 5 years old. Go now in your mind to that time, when you were this young child. For all moments in the past, the present and the future, coexist, they exist together, in the ever present NOW of your subconscious mind. So going there is really the same as coming here…to that part of your experience that is still a very young child.

Are you there yet? Good. Enjoy the sensations of awe and wonder, through the eyes of yourself as a young child. For young children know, don't they, that the imagination is a powerful thing, as powerful and real as anything you can touch or feel. You need only to look around you to realize the power of imagination. Everything you see, everything that is, at one time existed only in someone's imagination, CAME TO BE because of someone's powerful, creative imagination. So experience, now, the imagination of a young child, and recall to your mind a time or even when you were imagining, playing, as a young child, and experience again how very real this powerful imagination feels.

I f you can imagine it, you can achieve it. Perhaps you remember, playing with toys and with other children. Remember how real Santa Claus, or the Tooth Fairy, or some other important figure was to you, how REAL they were to you. There was no doubt, was there? Experience this now, the intense feeling, the reality of your powerful, creative mind. And simply believe. Look around you – who are you with? Bring them in, invite others to play with you. What do you see? Hear? Feel? Smell? Taste? Ahh, remember now, the smell of crayons! How real is that? And what IS real?

And just as your powerful imagination seemed real when you were a young child, it still has that power now…in this ever-present NOW, because then is now, and all experience is available to us at all times, and so we can bring that power of imagination forward in time with us now.

Imagine now, a time when you were not at all interested in eating, a time when you had no appetite, your hunger was just a whisper that spoke to you when you were truly hungry, when your body needed calories and nourishment. A time when you were completely comfortable and very easily satisfied with small amounts of food. A time when it was easy to make the right choice, because your appetite was not a factor. Perhaps this happened at a time when you were focusing intently on something, perhaps at work, or working on a hobby, maybe when you become completely engrossed in a good book, or while writing. Bring this into your imagination, and feel this pleasant, comfortable sensation of being neither hungry nor full. Your body feels just right. You are pleasantly engrossed in whatever task is at hand, and eating is the furthest thing from your mind.

Imagine now, as well, that you are feeling the most delightful sense of happiness, a powerful sense of well-being. Imagine now a time in your life when you felt such a feeling of happiness, of joy. Perhaps you just won an award or someone special did something wonderful for you. Imagine, and really feel, these positive emotions of happiness, almost a euphoria, a state of bliss. All is well with the world, all is well with you. Focus on how GOOD these emotions feel, and make them even stronger now. Twice as strong, now, stronger with every breath (etc.) one thousand times as strong now, as strong as you can possibly feel these wonderful feelings of happiness, joy, bliss, euphoria. And lock these feelings into your subconscious mind now.

As these feelings grow stronger and stronger, the feeling of being satisfied, of having no hunger, no appetite, becomes stronger and stronger….and as that feeling becomes stronger and stronger, your happiness, your euphoria grows and grows and so they grow together, like an endless feedback loop. And any time you want to feel this way, all you need to do is close your eyes, and visualize yourself swallowing a pill. This is your hypnotic diet pill, and it is the most powerful diet pill in the world. Do this now, imagine, visualize that you are picking up a pill in your hand, putting it in your mouth. See the glass of water there, pick it up and swallow this powerful diet pill. This pill takes away all appetite, all cravings for any type of unhealthy food.

Of course, when your body needs food for fuel, you will experience true hunger because your body requires nutrition and calories to maintain its functions; you will perceive that true, physical hunger. Your hunger will be mild, just enough to get your attention, and you will pay attention to this true hunger and honor this message from your body by providing it with clean, healthy, nutritious food, lean meats, fresh fruits and vegetables, and whole grains. You feed your body what it requires and needs for fuel, for proper nutrition, and for maintaining proper health while releasing extra unneeded fat. And your subconscious mind knows exactly how many calories are required and what level of physical activity is needed to reach your ideal weight, and so that behavior begins now. Everything you put into your body turns into health and perfection, or you would not put it into your mouth. You eat health, clean nutritious food only. You don't miss the junk food, the unhealthy food, the empty calorie food that you may have eaten in the past. You know that that kind of food is unhealthy for your body, and if you eat that kind of food, you will have unpleasant consequences.

And any time you want to feel this complete lack of appetite, all you need to do is close your eyes, and visualize yourself swallowing a pill. This is your hypnotic diet pill, and it is the most powerful diet pill in the world. Do this now, imagine, visualize that you are picking up a pill in your hand, putting it in your mouth. See the glass of water there, pick it up and swallow this powerful diet pill. This pill takes away all appetite, all cravings for any type of unhealthy food.

You find that you are craving water more and more. Only water truly satisfies your thirst, and so you find yourself reaching for water more and more frequently. Nothing quenches your thirst like water, and water makes your food taste so much better, it really brings out the flavors in the food. Your habit now is to drink a glass of water before each meal, therefore, because the fresh, cold water cleanses your palate, makes the food taste so much better. You drink water with your meals and throughout your day, easily drinking 6,7, or 8 glasses of water or more each day.

And any time you want to feel this complete lack of appetite, all you need to do is close your eyes, and visualize yourself swallowing a pill. This is your hypnotic diet pill, and it is the most powerful diet pill in the world. Do this now, imagine, visualize that you are picking up a pill in your hand, putting it in your mouth. See the glass of water there, pick it up and swallow this powerful diet pill. This pill takes away all appetite, all cravings for any type of unhealthy food.

Imagine now that you are on a journey. Picture or imagine yourself starting down a beautiful road, with lush green plants along the road, beautiful flowers everywhere. Things are growing and blooming, setting fruit, and health and beauty abounds. You are in the natural state of things. A little ways down the road you must make a decision, a choice, to take a path that leads to the left, or a path that leads to the right. The path leading to the left slopes slightly downhill, and then curves, so that you cannot see around the bend. As you look down the path, you see that there are fewer plants as the path goes on, and they don't seem to be as healthy. The path to the right goes slightly uphill, but the plants seem much healthier as far as the eye can see. Still, because it looks easier, you choose the path on the left. Everyone who walks along this path is asked to pay a toll, and to take a bucket and water the plants along the road. You begin down the road and quickly come to the first toll booth. The cost is not much, so you pay the toll and are given a bucket of water and asked to water the plants. You look into the bucket and see that the water has a slight skim of grease or oil on top of it, and a bit of an unpleasant smell. But the road is an easy one, so you decide to water the plants and continue on your way.

Further down the path you reach a second toll booth. At this booth, the toll has increased. It is double the cost of the first toll. Still, the path slopes downhill and seems easy, so you pay your toll. You are given a bucket of water and again are asked to water the plants. You look into this bucket and see not only a skim of grease or fat, but some other bits of stuff floating in it. There is a distinct bad odor to the water, and you notice that the plants here are decidedly less healthy than they were at the first toll. Still, the path does go downhill and seems easy, so you water the plants and continue on your way.

A bit further down the path you come to a third toll booth. The toll here is significantly higher than the first one—it is expensive enough that it makes you hesitate. But after all, you have already come this far, and the path seems easy. However, at this toll booth the guard also informs you that in order to continue, you must not only water the plants but you must wear a ball and chain around your ankle. You look at the bucket and it is full of sludge, it stinks, it does not even resemble water. You pick up the ball and chain. It will be quite a burden and you realize that even though the path has seemed to be easy, you have in fact been paying a heavy price, and this burden will slow your progress terribly. Why, it would have been easier, in fact, to take the road to the right, the road that went slightly uphill. You close your eyes and wish that you could be back at the fork in the road. You wish that you could choose the path to the right.

When you open your eyes again, your wish has been granted, and you are at the fork in the road. Although this path goes slightly uphill, you are happy to be on this path. It is so lush and green and healthy, as far as the eye can see. A little ways down the road you reach the first toll booth. The toll is very cheap, and you pay it gladly. You are given a bucket of clean, clear, fresh water to water the beautiful green, healthy plants. You water them gladly, and continue on your way.

Soon you reach the second toll booth, and you realize that even though the path is an upward one, it is in fact no more difficult and in many ways easier than the downhill path. At the second checkpoint, the toll is the same price as the first one, and the bucket of water is again clean, clear and fresh. The plants are beautiful and you notice for the first time that there are other people also walking this path. You admire them, they seem so healthy, and there is a spring in their steps. They look so happy.

At the third toll booth you pay the small toll and receive your bucket of clean, fresh water. At this toll booth the guard points to your leg. You look down and notice the ball and chain around your ankle. You have been carrying it since you were on the downhill path, the path to the left. But somehow it looks different now. It is smaller, lighter. The guard tells you that at this checkpoint the burden may now be removed, and smiling, you reach down and easily pull the chain off of your ankle, leaving it behind.

Your step is now light, you have a spring in your step that you noticed in the other people along this path. A little ways down the path you come to a beautiful reflecting pool. You look into the pool and see your reflection and you smile. You are now just like those other people, light, glowing with health, at your perfect weight. You are now on the right path, and you promise yourself never to leave it.

Nighttime Weight Release

About the script

This script has no trance termination. It is designed to be recorded for your client to listen to as they fall asleep. It is truly just an extended progressive relaxation, with suggestions distributed throughout the progression. As such, there is no induction required; the script is complete in and of itself.

Script: *Nighttime Weight Release*

This meditation is designed to be heard just as you are going to sleep. You should be comfortably lying down in your bed, you should have your eyes closed and you also should be in deep and exhaling in a relaxed rhythmic fashion.

In this moment begin to envision your day tomorrow, imagine exactly how it is going to go tomorrow when you wake up. Picture yourself achieving every single task or goal you have lined up for you your day and what experiences you would like to have. See how you are being absolutely successful in every aspect of your life. If you are working on positive attributes and habits, see how you are doing them all tomorrow with the greatest of ease. Envision the time that you are going to wake up, see how you open your eyes in the morning completely refreshed and energized, ready to take on your day.

(Pause)

In this next moment start imagining your ideal body, just simply relax and let go of everything. See how you resemble the exact image you have in your mind and how you feel wonderful about it. Imagine yourself enjoying every aspect of your healthy body, feel how good it feels to be fit.

Maintain that image in your head and allow yourself to completely relax, melt away and let go of everything else. Simply listen to the sound of my voice. Take in a deep breath and hold it (slight pause) now exhale and feel how complete relaxation slowly covers your entire mind and body.

Deep inside your subconscious there is a part that knows exactly what you need to do in order for you to lose weight easily and completely naturally. All that is required of you at this point in time is for you to relax and to allow your body to do its job, notice how a calm wave of relaxation covers your body from head to toe. Beginning with the forehead, feel how it is relaxing at this moment, completely letting go of all tension and becoming comfortably limp. As you feel your forehead releasing all tension, all stress and strain and confusion complete evaporates. You have a clear and relaxed state of mind. You are so relaxed at this moment, and any outside noise only motivates you to go deeper into sleep, relaxed and giving your mind the power to literally create the body you desire…your perfect body. While maintaining this perfect body in your mind, feel how the relaxation moves from your forehead and into your face. Feel how all your facial muscles completely relax and go completely loose. There is only a complete sense of relaxation over your entire head.

Feel how all the tendons around your eyes go limp and relaxed. It becomes so relaxed that you can soon become aware that you can physically feel positive shifts happening inside your body. Your body is becoming comfortable with completely letting go and giving your mind absolute control over every aspect within your body. Simply by breathing in a relaxed position your body now begins to release all excess weight. Feel how it just melts off your body, feel how it becomes less and less every single day. All this is happening simply because you are letting go, which is very easy and natural for you to do. You simply let go of all thoughts, you let go of all worry and care, you evaporate all concerns for the day.

Begin to feel how your neck is becoming more relaxed, how all the muscles simply become limp. Your neck, face and head are all now in a complete state of relaxation. Your entire head and neck are so relaxed that each time you listen to this meditation your mind instantly becomes calm, and very focused. Your mind also realizes that it is confident that every waking moment of your life you are losing weight naturally and effortlessly, and finding success in every aspect of your life.

Feel how your shoulders go completely limp and relaxed, how the pure power of calmness covers you. You are starting to understand that something inside of you is changing, life is getting better and better, it becomes easier and requires less effort to do. Each passing day only gets easier and much better, filled with purpose and meaning; smile as you realize that your life is fun, exciting and is so satisfying to you.

You feel the relaxed feeling touch your upper arms and elbows making them go completely relaxed and comfortable. Your mind is open to the transformation that is taking place in this very instant, how you are losing weight without any trouble, quickly and automatically. Your body is in complete and perfect harmony, only using what it needs and expelling everything else. You have a smaller appetite, a healthy one that gives you more energy than ever before. This energy impulse you to live life to the fullest, all you crave are healthy foods full of nutrients and vitamins that will only help your body succeed. Your body has supreme wisdom and intelligence and understands that it is in your best interest to be healthy and on your ideal weight. Your body craves to be healthy and thin, and so you begin to lose weight easily and naturally, stress free and with a passionate drive to be at your ideal weight. So you can relax completely, and the more you relax now the easier it is to lose weight when you wake up.

Begin to notice how your elbows, forearms and even your fingers are completely melting away under the powerful relaxation that is covering your body. It is so relaxed and at ease that everything you need to lose weight will come to you easily. As easy as it is breathing the air that is filling your lungs at this very moment. All you need to do is breathe this state into reality and it must obey. Every time you listen to this meditation you become much more relaxed than the previous time, you are learning to allow your body to take care of itself, to allow healing energy to cover you in every cell, stating the exact same message of health and happiness. This state is enhancing your life in this very moment, all your relationships and thoughts are being affected by it for the better, molding your perfect body and mind.

The deeper you drift into this state of pure relaxation the greater control you have over your life in every waking second and the easier it becomes to automatically release all excess unwanted weight. You are amazed at how quickly you are losing weight, and you are overjoyed that your body is doing all this work for you without requiring any effort. You become less hungry and only crave things that benefit your body and health; foods that are there to enhance your life. You begin to feel the same energy you had as a child coming back, wanting to help you achieve your goals. You begin to have a desire to do physical activities when you are awake, running, biking, walking on the beach, surfing or swimming. In the morning you will have a deep desire to burn all the energy of your youth, your body craves it.

Begin to feel your chest and abdomen and back relax completely, melting away all tension allowing your mind to have even more control, to be even more receptive and even more empowered to change your physical condition. All changes that benefit you, your mind, your habits, your food preferences, your energy levels and all thoughts and feelings. Everything works in unison to make you the perfect version of you. It allows you to eliminate all stress, fear and confusion and replaces it all with only good things for your mind and body. You have already made the decision to better your life, and now your body and mind are both responding, working nonstop to achieve your vision, your goal. All you need to do is take deep long breathes in and exhale all negative feelings. Every time you do this you go much deeper than before, you become much more relaxed and your mind and body is absolutely open and receptive. You feel how you are obtaining a greater sense of control, and you know it will be in full throttle when you wake up in the morning.

Each positive thought begins to saturate your mind. You begin to feel your hips and gluteus relax. Begin to feel how relaxed every cell in your body is, how every organ is completely and utterly in sync with your state of calmness and relaxation. Feel how it improves your circulation, allowing all good things to flow all over your body, bringing life to each organ and effortlessly allowing you to lose weight every day. See yourself getting thinner each and every day, becoming much more fit and reaching your ideal weight without any interference. Your body doesn't need to hold on to any excess weight, it is satisfied with the food you give it, food is abundant and always available…so there is no need for it. Your body realizes that there is no reason to store any extra calories in your body, there is always food when you need it.

Your body is losing weight because now it is easy to do, and there is no need to store food in your body. There is no need to have weight to protect you, you are completely safe and sheltered. Everybody is in charge of their own lives and you know this, so you can relax and let go of all worries. Everyone around you is only giving you positive energy that aids you in your life. All these people will nourish you and support you, they love to help you out. They all changed around you because you have taken the first step, you are more positive and vibrant than ever and this is affecting all your relationships for the better. All these changes happened because you have decided, you have commanded your body and mind to follow your plan to the letter.

Continue now to breathe in deeply and allow all fat to melt off of your body. There is no resistance because you have commanded your powerful mind to do the rest. Your mind is transforming you into the ideal version of you. Feel how your body is burning the fat, making it melt of because it doesn't need it anymore, your body wants to be in shape and healthy. All your body desires is to be healthy and fit, to have that ideal weight, it is a strong desire from both your mind and body. The deeper you drift into relaxation, the more open your mind is and the faster it responds.

Your mind and body is open to getting healthy and rich foods that benefit and energizes your body. These foods become better tasting every passing day, they all satisfy your body with their wonderful vitamins and nutrients. You no longer have a desire to eat things that don't benefit your body, all fast food and soft drinks become nothing more than cardboard to you. Your body repels all these chemicals, it only desires good things.

All you want is good healthy foods, you enjoy chewing them thoroughly and eat them slowly. Every bite you savor the taste, understanding what it does to your body…how it assists in every possible way. You have the perfect balance in nourishing your body, mind and complete being.

Now as you take another deep breath you begin to feel how the pure power of relaxation flows to your knees and legs. Feel how they go completely limp and relaxed and know that all changes that you desire are already happening in a natural and automatic fashion. You begin to desire healthy things like drinking water instead of soda, eating nutritious foods instead of junk, being active and feeling completely satisfied with life. All these thoughts and feeling all work together to simply allow the weight to melt off of your body, changing your life for the better.

Every single aspect of your life is changing, improving and creating a new freshness in your life. Your life is filled with wonderful opportunities and you embrace every single one of them, living to the max. There is a sense of newness inside of you, each day becoming better than the one before. You begin to see the world with new eyes, a fresh perspective of everything around you. You become happier with every waking day, knowing that good things are coming your way, relaxed and knowing that your body is doing all the work, you simply have to allow it. Your body wants to be thin; it is thin and is working to maintain that thinness.

Losing your weight is easy, very simple and requires no effort. It's so easy that you can actually feel the fat melting off of your body in this very instant. Feel how your body is letting go of every excess calorie that your body might be storing. You are beginning to realize that losing weight is much easier than you thought, you are redefining your mind. Feel how you are embracing life and this experience, how you are opening a new chapter in your life.

Begin to feel how the pure power of relaxation is reaching your feet and toes. Feel how they are all letting go simply drifting into a deep state of relaxation. In this moment simply take a moment to enjoy the full body state of relaxation you are experience in this moment. Even when you hear the sound of my voice it will only add to the state of pure relaxation making you calmer and deeper in your mind, more focused than ever. You are now ten times more relaxed, and you can only feel every breath you take a deeper sense of calmness and relaxation. When you hear my voice again you will be more capable of taking positive steps in reaching your ideal weight, your mind will be more open and you will be in the perfect state of synchronization with your body. (pause for 30 seconds)

You are more successful, more fulfilled and incredibly happy with every aspect of your life and every day you are becoming healthier and in better shape. Envision yourself as you want to be, feel the way you want to feel. Begin to see yourself as the best version, physically and emotionally that you have always desired. Your body and mind has now exactly matched itself with that image, it has anchored that state as a permanent state in your being. Now you find yourself less hungry day by day, you only crave healthy foods and your metabolism is perfect, burning all fat quickly and very easily.

You have much more energy and want to go out and experience life to the max. You are in love with the fact that you are healthy and physically attractive. You enjoy exercise and all of a sudden you feel overjoyed with life, loving every second of it. Exercise is one of your greatest expression of freedom and health, and you love it.

You are much stronger emotionally, physically and mentally. You easily find ways to protect yourself and don't allow others to affect your state of being. You are safe and life in all its aspects is safe as well. You have completely conditioned both your mind and body to be thin and healthy. Your body now allows you to lose weight effortlessly and knows that it is safe to be thin. You easily reach your goals. You release the past and let it go, exhaling every thought and bad experience. You move forward to your ideal weight and feel great doing it.

You find yourself more positive, a great attitude and just a joy for living. You know that life is a gift and you intend to live it to the fullest. Life only gets easier and easier day by day. You know that your body has the desire to be thin and is doing everything in its power to attain it. Your body and mind are incredibly powerful, and they both are working just for you.

As you drift off to sleep you begin to realize that tonight your body and your mind will be working. They will work nonstop until you have achieved the vision you have created. Every single night and every single day, every minute and second your body is working to reach and maintain your ideal weight forever. This happens without resistance, you can feel that this sleep will energize you and motivate you tomorrow. You allow yourself to be healthy and thin, you know it is safe to be thin, it's easy to be thin and your body craves it. Your body wants to be thin, it is thin and is working to show you. Now as you drift into the calmness of your subconscious, know that your body is working and that in this very moment…you are reaching your ideal weight.

Natural Weight Release

About the script

This is a good, foundational weight release script. While other scripts may be required either separately or incorporated with this script for ego strengthening, this script covers the bases of ensuring that the subconscious mind understands, accepts and implements the behavioral changes required to release excess body weight. It is provided complete with induction and trance termination, although you may certainly substitute your own preferred methods.

Script: Natural Weight Release

Sit or lie back, find yourself in a relaxing position. Close your eyes and breathe comfortably.

Relax.

Begin by taking a deep breath in through your nose, hold it for the mental count of 3, and exhale slowly through your mouth.

Again. Breathing in peace and comfort, breathing out all stress and tension. Just letting go.

And one more time. Feel the body begin to relax. As the body relaxes, the mind slows. And as the mind slows, the body relaxes. Every breath you take continues to relax you even further.

Letting go.

Notice how relaxed your body is beginning to feel, and you wonder to yourself how much more relaxed you can become.

Allowing yourself this time for you. Giving yourself permission to enter the hypnotic state.

Every breath continuing to relax you even further; relaxing even further with every number I count backwards from 5 to 0. Every number I count backwards from 5 to 0 representing a deeper level of relaxation; a deeper level of hypnosis.

5   4   3   2   1   0   0   0

Zero is deep sleep. Deeeeep sleep. Letting go.

Imagine now comfortable waves of relaxation flowing over your body. Picture, imagine them in your mind. Flowing waves of relaxation beginning at the top of your head, and flowing through your body, to the tips of your toes. Every muscle is touched by these waves of relaxation, and every muscle that is touched relaxes totally and completely. Letting go.

Perhaps these waves of relaxation have a color. Picture, visualize, imagine them now in your mind, these colorful waves of relaxation, flowing from the top of your head, touching every muscle in your body, all the way down to your toes. Imagine the waves starting at the crown of your head, relaxing your scalp muscles, the muscles in the back of your head and your temples. Imagine them relaxing your face muscles, your forehead relaxing and smoothing out; the small muscles around your eyes; the bridge of your nose, your cheeks and jaw. Your jaw relaxing and letting go, leaving perhaps a small gap between your teeth. Your neck relaxing, and your shoulders become loose, sinking a little further down. Letting go.

The wave coming down your arms now, your biceps and triceps, elbows, forearms, wrists, hands and fingers. Even the spaces between your fingers feeling totally relaxed. Every muscle in your body now beginning to feel like a handful of loose, limp, rubber bands.

Feel the wave flowing down your spine, the muscles on either side of your spine; your upper, middle, and lower back releasing all tension, letting go. Your chest and stomach muscles relaxing, as every breath continues to take you deeper. Your waist and hips letting go and your body sinks down even more deeply. Every muscle feeling like a wet, limp, dishrag, or a plate of jello.

Your upper legs, knees, shins and calves, ankles and feet relaxing. The tops of the feet, and the soles of the feet, your heels, arches, balls of the feet and toes. And even the spaces between your toes.

Scan your body lightly for any remaining sources of tension and if you find any simply acknowledge it, release it and let it go.

Every breath continues to relax the body further, and as the body relaxes, the mind slows, and as the mind slows, the body relaxes. Going deeper.

Going even deeper into relaxation, even deeper into hypnosis with every number that I count from 5, 4, 3, 2, 1, 0   0   0 is deeeep sleep. Deeeeeep sleep. And every time I count from 5 to 0 and say the words deep sleep, with your permission and for the purpose of hypnosis, you will reach this level of hypnosis or deeper, quickly and easily. Letting go.

Thoughts may come and thoughts may go in hypnosis. If you have a thought simply acknowledge it, release it and let it go, knowing that at all times your subconscious mind is focused on the sound of my voice.

You may hear sounds in the room or building around you while you are in hypnosis. Any sounds you hear are only the sounds of every day life, and cannot distract or disturb you, but will only cause you to go deeper and deeper.

If for any reason, such as an emergency, you <u>need</u> to awaken while listening to this recording, you will come to a full waking state feeling calm and relaxed, knowing exactly what to do.

Now let's proceed.

As you continue to relax further with every breath, knowing that your subconscious mind is focused on the sound of my voice, and is accepting these suggestions for positive change, positive change that you desire. For you desire now to release the extra weight you have been carrying for so long. You desire to reclaim your right to be healthier in all ways, mentally, physically, emotionally and spiritually. And because you desire this change, all parts of you accept these suggestions. These suggestions become stronger and stronger, more and more effective every day, and every time you listen to this recording.

You desire positive change in your life now, you desire to lose the extra weight. You want the wonderful benefits that come with having a fit, healthy body—the ability to do the activities you enjoy, the ability to resist illness, the feeling that comes with having a strong, healthy body that you are proud of. If there are any other benefits of reaching your ideal weight that you have in mind, think of them to yourself now, and I will be quiet for a moment.

Pause

You have made a decision. You have reached a fork in the road and have made a decision. You know that your future health will be decided by the choices you make now. Picture, visualize or imagine yourself now standing at a fork in the road. One path leads to your left, the other to your right. Down the path to the left is your life if you do not take control of your eating and exercise, to reach your healthy, ideal weight. Down the path to the right, is your life when you commit to these positive changes, losing the extra weight, and keeping it off, for good.

Let's imagine that 5, 10, 15 years have gone by now, and you chose the path on the left. Imagine the months and the years going by as you project your mind into the future. Fifteen years have gone by, and you chose not to change your eating and exercising behavior. Fifteen years have gone by, and you are still heavy, perhaps heavier, paying the price for your decision not to act. Imagine that there is a full-length mirror here in the road, 15 years in the future, and take a look at yourself. How do you look? How heavy, or how much heavier are you? What is your health like? Your skin and muscle tone? Can you do the things you want to? How has this decision affected every aspect of your life, your health, your relationships, your career and your personal life? Can you live with THIS decision?

Now leave that image and come back to the present day, the present time. Back to the fork in the road. Back to the decision you face. And now imagine that 5, 10, 15 years have gone by and you chose the path on the right. The path of deciding to take control of your eating and exercise behavior, the path to losing the weight and reaching and maintaining your ideal weight. There once again is that full-length mirror. Go ahead and take a look. How do you look 15 years in the future down THIS path? How fit and healthy are you? Look at how well you have maintained your weight loss and your health. How good your skin tone and your muscle tone is. How you enjoy doing any activity you want to. How has this decision to take control of your health affected every aspect of your life, your health, your relationships, your career and personal life? It is clear now which decision you are making. You have already MADE your decision, haven't you?

Now let that image fade…let it fade and go deeper now with 5, 4, 3,2,1,0 0   0 is deep sleep etc.

Picture, visualize or imagine yourself now, with all the weight gone. All the weight that you want to lose. And imagine yourself in front of a full length mirror. Look at yourself closely from the front, back and sides, visualizing yourself with all the weight gone. You are at your perfect weight. You have done it, you have lost all the weight that you want to lose. How does this make you feel? Happy? Proud, full of joy for your accomplishment. Feel the sense of achievement, the self-confidence. Really get in touch with these feelings, and with every breath allow these feelings to grow stronger and stronger.

Twice as strong now.

Ten times as strong now.

One hundred times as strong now. Stronger with every breath, these positive feelings of confidence, pride and accomplishment. One thousand times as strong now, as strong as you can possibly feel them. Now lock these feelings into your subconscious mind as this becomes the blueprint for the new you. This is now your unconscious self image, a healthy, fit you, at your ideal weight.

Now picture, visualize or imagine yourself eating the right foods, the healthy choices-lean meats, vegetables and fruits, whole grain breads and cereals, in smaller amounts. Each time you make these healthy food choices, the subconscious self image of you at your ideal weight grows stronger and stronger, and as the subconscious image of yourself at your ideal weight grows stronger, you make more and more healthy eating choices. These feelings now reinforce each other and themselves, in an endless circle of health.

And naturally because you like and love yourself and your body, you do everything to maintain this beautiful new you. Everything you eat and drink, everything you do, increases the health and perfection of your body, or you would not eat it, drink it or do it. The subconscious motivation to maintain this ideal self-image grows stronger and stronger every day, and as it grows stronger the desire to eat in a healthy way grows stronger and stronger. And this is so.

You find yourself naturally eating smaller and smaller portions, and making healthy, slimming choices-lean meats, fruits and vegetables, whole grains. You find you have no appetite for foods that cause you to remain overweight, the fatty foods, the sweet foods, the starchy foods. You have no appetite for them and in fact, because you know they threaten your self-image of yourself at your ideal weight, you avoid them. You know that if you eat these foods, there will be unpleasant consequences for you.

You find yourself reaching more and more often for fresh, cold water. Nothing quenches your thirst as well as water, and your body craves more and more water, drinking plenty of it each day. In fact, water is now your beverage of choice, and you choose water over all other drinks. You find that water makes your food taste better, cleans the palate and makes your food taste really good. So you drink a glass of water before every meal, because it makes the food taste that much better. You drink water with your meals, stopping between bites to take a drink of water.

Picture, visualize or imagine yourself now, sitting down to a meal. There is a buffet, a choice of foods in front of you. There are all sorts of foods here, all kinds of choices. You find yourself drawn to the healthy choices. Look carefully at what you are choosing to put on your plate. Lean meats, fresh vegetables and fruits, and whole grains. Others around you are making poor choices. Look at their plates, heaped up with starches and fats, and sweets. And look at them. They are overweight, their bodies reflect the food choices that they are making. We really are what we eat.

Picture yourself now sitting down to enjoy your meal. As always now, you drink a glass of water before your meal, because water enhances the taste of your food, making the flavors stronger, better. This makes you feel more satisfied. You eat a small amount of healthy, nutritious food, and you find that you feel totally satisfied both physically and emotionally from a small amount of healthy, nutritious food. You are now very in tune with your true hunger, and only eat when the body is truly hungry, not out of emotional reasons.

As you get in touch with your hunger, you imagine it as a scale from 1 to 10, much like the fuel tank in a car. At 1 or 2, you are hungry. At 5 or 6, you have that comfortable, warm feeling that tells you that you have eaten enough food to satisfy the needs of your body. Eating beyond 6 on the scale, eating to a 7, 8, 9 or 10 on the scale makes you feel physically uncomfortable, and brings unpleasant consequences.

And you only pay attention to true hunger, which comes from the stomach, behind the rib cage, above the belly button. And so at 1 or 2 on the scale you choose to eat, selecting a small amount of healthy, nutritious food. You drink a glass of water before your meal and you eat slowly, taking the time to really enjoy the flavor of each bite. You set your fork down in between bites, and occasionally drink water throughout your meal. You check in with your hunger scale, or fuel gauge, every couple of bites. You pay attention as you move from a 1 or 2, to a 2 or 3 or 4 on the scale, knowing that each bite brings you closer to 5 or 6 on the scale. When you reach 5 or 6 on the scale, you stop eating, knowing that you have eaten enough healthy, nutritious food to satisfy your body, enough healthy, nutritious food to maintain that beautiful self image of yourself at your ideal weight. If there is food left on your plate when you reach 5 or 6 on the scale, you feel completely comfortable leaving it there, knowing that eating any further will bring unpleasant consequences.

Going deeper now with 5, 4, 3, 2, 1, 0 0   0 is deep sleep. DEEEEEEEP sleep. And every time I count from 5 to 0 and say the words deep sleep, with your permission and for the purpose of hypnosis, you will reach this level of hypnosis or deeper, quickly and easily.

Recall to mind now that image of yourself at your ideal weight, that image of yourself from the front, back and sides with all the extra weight gone. Your ideal weight. Really picture this image in your mind. Your subconscious mind knows exactly what to do and how to behave to reach and maintain this ideal weight, and it begins now to create those behaviors and attitudes in you, to create this new reality for you now.

Any old feelings or beliefs that kept you from achieving this goal in the past are being eliminated now. And we are going to eliminate them with an orange healing light. Every cell, fiber in your body, every thought, memory and belief in your mind will be changed and healed by this orange healing light. Picture in your mind now a glass bottle, shaped exactly like you. And at the bottom of this bottle, in the toes, are valves through which this healing light enters. The healing light comes into the YOU-shaped bottle from the toes, and fills the body, up from the toes, the legs, the knees, the thighs, hips and waist, up your chest, shoulders and filling your head. Every cell, every fiber in your body is now being healed, every thought, memory and belief is being changed by this orange, healing light. All of your being, physically, mentally and emotionally is now being aligned with the your positive new self-image, the image of yourself at your ideal weight. Any negative thought or belief that, in the past, prevented you from achieving your goal of permanent weight loss is now being eliminated. Every cell in your body is being changed, to increase the elimination of fat from the body, to turn the body into a being of health and perfection. Picture, visualize or imagine the orange healing light filling and shining out from every part of the YOU-shaped bottle, as this healing change takes place, changing you physically, emotionally, mentally and spiritually, completely aligning you with your new, healthy self-image. Really FEEL the orange, healing light bringing positive change to every part of your body and your mind. And every part of you accepts this change because this is positive change that you desire. Any thought, memory or belief that, in the past, prevented you from achieving this goal has been eliminated, and they are in the past now, over and done. You are moving forward on your path to permanent weight loss, to achieving your ideal weight. And your subconscious mind knows EXACTLY what actions and behaviors are required to achieve that goal, and implements those behaviors and actions NOW, to bring about this new you, quickly and easily.

Let that image fade now, let it fade, and go deeper with 5, 4, 3, 2, 1, 0 0 0 etc.

Picture, visualize or imagine yourself now at the top of a safe, well-let staircase of 20 steps. And at the bottom of this staircase lies your goal of permanent weight loss, your goal of achieving your ideal weight.

Allow your creative subconscious mind to choose a symbol or an image now that represents this goal, and see that symbol or image at the bottom of this staircase. Every step down the staircase represents a step closer and closer to your goal, until at last, at the bottom of the staircase you reach your goal. And as you reach your goal here, in the safety of hypnosis, so you will reach your goal in your waking state, quickly and easily. So let's begin, starting with your left foot at 19, 18, etc. 0, you have reached your goal. Reach out and claim it, take it, own it in whatever way makes sense to you. And as you have achieved your goal here, in the safety of hypnosis, so you will achieve your goal in your waking state, quickly and easily.

These suggestions grow stronger and stronger, more and more effective each and every day. Every part of you accepts these suggestions, as these are suggestions for positive change which you desire.

So the benefits will be multiplied upon awakening, I say to you now, if this is a time and a place where you need to be awake, alert, and conscious, then you will slowly find yourself returning back into the room as I count up from 1 to 5...slowly finding yourself returning back into the room where your eyes will open, you will become wide awake...feeling fine and in perfect health...feeling better than ever before, perhaps feeling as if you've just returned from a deep, relaxing, powerful mental holiday. 1 2 3   4 5 Eyes open, wide awake.

Confidence for Weight Release

About the script

An accompanying script for weight release, this is designed to instill an "I can do it" attitude and boost of confidence. It's appropriate for those clients who perhaps have always been heavy and are unsure of their body's ability to release weight, and/or their abilities to change their behaviors.

Script: Confidence for Weight Release

USE YOUR PREFERRED INDUCTION METHOD

And as you go even deeper, listening to the sound of my voice, you begin to think about a time when you felt very confident, completely confident and in control. Think of that time now, a time in your life, or a situation, when you felt completely confident, completely in control. Begin to feel those feelings even more strongly, feeling strong, feeling in control, taking control. Let those feelings grow stronger and stronger now with every breath, becoming twice as strong.....ten times as strong....continuing to grow stronger with every breath, one hundred times as strong, a thousand times as strong, as strong as you can possibly feel these positive feelings of confidence and control. And lock those feelings of confidence and control into your subconscious mind, as your new self image, as this confident you, completely in control.

And now picture, visualize or imagine yourself now, with all the weight gone. All the weight that you want to lose is gone. And imagine yourself in front of a full length mirror. Look at yourself closely from the front, back and sides, visualizing yourself with all the weight gone. You are at your perfect weight. You have done it, you have lost all the weight that you want to lose. How does this make you feel? Happy? Proud? Full of joy for your accomplishment. Feel the sense of achievement, the satisfaction, the pride. Really get in touch with these feelings, and with every breath allow these feelings to grow stronger and stronger. And as these feelings grow stronger, the feelings of confidence and control grow stronger. And as your feelings of confidence and control grow stronger, the feelings of accomplishment and pride at reaching your goal of permanent weight loss grow stronger and stronger.

You have all the confidence you need, to become this new you, your ideal self at your ideal weight. You and you alone have your best interests at heart, and you now take control of your life. You trust your own judgement in all things and you know that you alone have your best interests at heart. This decision to lose the extra weight is completely within your control, and that knowledge brings a great sense of confidence and a sense of peace, because you know that YOU CAN DO IT. You find it easy to concentrate on what is important to you, and this goal is important to you. Your subconscious mind helps you in all ways, reminding you of your positive qualities. You notice that others around you appreciate you more as you become more positive, more self-confident, happier and your confidence grows and manifests itself in your day-to-day success, not only in becoming your ideal weight, but in other ways as well, ways that you may imagine in your mind now....

You can now be aware that you have all the capabilities you need, all the strengths, all the qualities, all the skills and knowledge required to meet your goal of reaching your ideal weight. You are realizing that now every day with greater clarity each and every day. And you can unlearn those old feelings of fear and lack of confidence, lack of self control. You know take a deep breath, relaxing your body and mind, and take the image of your mind into you, happy and secure, confident and self-assured, self-controlled. As you tell yourself I CAN.....I WILL... and this comfortable, pleasant image soothes your mind, replacing any sense of fear or self doubt as all negative emotions leave you completely.

You unlearn any old patterns of lack of confidence, lack of self control. You unlearn these by being positive and by realizing that the only thing that can hurt you is fear itself. And you no longer accept fear or negativity, you banish them in their entirety, along with any inappropriate thoughts... allowing only good thoughts and positive feelings of confidence and self control to grow and become a permanent part of your self image. You do this easily and you do this by releasing the old negative thoughts and the old negative self image now, as one releases a helium balloon, watching it become smaller and smaller in the sky, until it is gone completely.

And now, Visualize, imagine or just pretend that you are at an outdoor party. Perhaps it is for you, or someone close to you. You see a large bundle of brightly colored helium balloons in front of you.

Reaching down, you pick up the first balloon which is a bright blue color, and as you look at it, you notice that it has some writing on it. Stretching it between your fingers you notice that it has a negative emotion written on it. You realize that this negative emotion is something that you have felt in the past, and that has been tied to your over-eating.

Perhaps it is a lack of self control, or a lack of confidence, or old habits. Perhaps it is an emotion that, in the past, triggered an emotional desire to eat, like sadness or anger.

These are emotions that you do not want to experience very often… and that you wish to be in control of. So thinking of these emotions, in your mind re-live a recent situation where you felt these emotions very strongly. Place yourself back into that situation – see the other individuals who might be there; see them looking at you as you were feeling these emotions; hear what you are saying; feel what you are feeling with great intensity; see the expression on your own face…and when you again feel the intensity of these negative emotions, simply release the balloon into the air, let go of the balloon and let go of these negative emotions, these negative behaviors and watch the helium balloon go up and up and up and up, into their air, further and further away, so far away that you can barely feel it, so far away …until it is gone forever. As you watch the balloon disappear say to yourself "I AM FREE!"

Let this image go and now go deeper with 5, 4, 3, 2, 1 etc.

Picture, visualize or imagine now that you're standing in a large and beautiful room - over there is a door and in a moment I'm going to ask you to walk over to the door and push it open - and when you do you'll find yourself in your favorite place and you'll be very happy to be there.

When you're ready - walk over to the door - push the door open - push - and the door opens easily for you - now walk through - closing the door gently behind you - and look around you - you are back here in your favorite place and it looks exactly the same as did when you came here last - it's a wonderful, sunshiny day and there's a clear blue sky and you feel so happy to be back here.

This is your perfect place - your paradise - and I want you to know that you can come back here anytime you want to - any time you want - all with the power of your wonderful subconscious mind. All you need to do is relax - and take three deep breaths - hold each one for the mental count of three - and as you breathe the air from your mouth - just think in your mind the words 'calm and relaxed' and you will instantly feel much calmer and much more relaxed - and more confident too.

Now - in your perfect place - I want you to create a circle around you - and you are standing or sitting here - in the center of your circle - this is your circle - your circle of excellence - your circle of confidence - your perfect circle.

And as you sit or stand in the center of your circle - I want you picture, visualize or imagine that you have lost all the weight that you want to lose, all the weight that you have been carrying. You have reached your ideal weight. Here is a full length mirror, and look at yourself from the front, back and sides. Get a really good look at yourself, and notice how good you feel. How self confident you feel. How wonderful you look and how confident and in-control you feel.

I'd like you to now allow your mind to create symbols or images for each of these feelings, these feelings of confidence, pride, accomplishment, self control and any other positive feelings that you are experiencing - and put those symbols into your circle - perhaps you can imagine writing them on the ground or in the sand - or maybe they're floating around you - making you feel really happy, really confident - as though you are floating on air yourself - and I'm going to be quiet for a few moments to allow you to create these symbols and feel those good feelings again - and put them all into your circle of excellence - your perfect circle - your circle of confidence.

I'll be quiet now - and when you next hear my voice you won't be startled or alarmed.

(Pause for two minutes)

Now - bring your attention back to my voice - because I want you to know and to understand that you can experience these good feelings again - whenever you want to - whenever you need to - all with the power of your own wonderful subconscious mind.

All you need to do is relax - and let go of tension - take those three deep breaths - hold each one for the mental count of three - and as you breathe out - think those words in your mind - calm and relaxed - and as you think those words in your mind you will find that you do become much more calm - and more relaxed - and much more confident too - and when you've said the words ' calm and relax' three times - I'd like you to think in your mind - my circle - just those two little words will instantly fill you with feelings of confidence and all the wonderful feelings and thoughts associated with your circle will be back in your awareness - even more powerful that they are right now.

The words - my circle - are your post hypnotic conditioned response - and when you're relaxing - in your own special time - you can go back into your circle - and you may find new things to add to it - there will be other feelings springing to mind - and new experiences resulting from your newly found confidence - and you can add them to your circle of confidence - this will help to make it even stronger and more powerful for you.

And what you put into your circle - you can use - you can take those confident feelings wherever you go - whenever you need them. Imagine yourself in a situation which, in the past, you would have felt out of control and would have over eaten or eaten out of an emotional need- and see yourself now doing or saying or whatever it is - with these wonderful feelings of confidence - calm and happiness. And notice the difference. Now you find it easy to eat smaller amounts, to eat healthy, nutritious food in smaller amounts, to exercise more frequently and with more intensity, as it is healthful for you, at all times maintaining good health. Your new self image of yourself at your ideal weight, healthy, confident, with great self-control.

Your wonderful subconscious mind accepts all of these suggestions, and these suggestions grow stronger and stronger, more and more effective each and every day, and this is so. Every part of your mind accepts these suggestions, because they are for your greater good. Your creative subconscious mind knows exactly the actions and behaviors required to become your ideal weight, and does so now with renewed and expanded confidence and self-control, creating the new, ideal you quickly and easily.

So the benefits will be multiplied upon awakening, I say to you now, if this is a time and a place where you need to be awake, alert, and conscious, then you will slowly find yourself returning back into the room as I count up from 1 to 5...slowly finding yourself returning back into the room where your eyes will open, you will become wide awake...feeling fine and in perfect health...feeling better than ever before, perhaps feeling as if you've just returned from a deep, relaxing, powerful mental holiday. 1 2 3   4 5 Eyes open, wide awake.

Part 3: Scripts for Improving Libido

Drive Your Desire

About the script

This script is written to instill confidence in men, that they are desirable, worthy of a woman's attention and an excellent lover.

Script: Drive Your Desire

USE YOUR PREFERRED INDUCTION METHOD

Now that you are in a complete state of peace and serenity you realize that you are standing in a room with several mirrors facing you from all sides. In the middle of this room is a large bed, your bed. You realize that this is your room of power and masculinity. This is where all your strength and your desire come to.

Take a moment to feel the power of this room, feel the sexual energy that is drifting in the air. Here you are on top of your game. There is no woman you cannot seduce; there is no woman that will leave this place without experiencing pleasure from you over and over again. In this place you are king supreme and there is no greater lover in your midst.

You are secure, in charge, comfortable with your body. You are powerful, and know exactly what to do to inspire hot passionate feelings in your partner(s). But more than just physical security you know that you are able to push all the right buttons and you can perceive in your lover's movements what is needed for greater pleasure. You are masterful.

WAIT 10 SECONDS

Imagine that on the bed is a beautiful woman waiting for you. She needs you to satisfy her needs and only you can do it. This woman can be anyone you desire, anyone you want. As you approach the bed you see her naked body calling you out, needing your touch.

You start off slow and run your fingers up her thighs, gently kiss her on the lips, then the breasts. You make her want you more; you make her crawl out of her skin. She needs you, she needs your firm hands to caress her all over, to release her from her own desires.

Take a moment to reflect on how you are feeling. Take a moment to notice how you seducing her is intensifying the sexual vibe in the atmosphere. You can look at the mirror in front of you. See the reflection, see how you are in complete control, see how she is in desperate need of you. Remember this feeling, remember this moment. You can access this at any time, you can use this anytime you desire. Remember this feeling right now.

WAIT 10 SECONDS

You now continue, etching slower towards full satisfaction. Listen to her breathing, listen to her yearning. Feel her skin; be in the moment right now. See how the two of you are connecting in a way you have never felt before; she has never felt this before either. Only you managed to read her perfectly, to touch just the right buttons and to make her want you more than anything on this planet.

Know that you have this power to read women, to know what they want, to satisfy their desires. You are subtle and gentle but firm and powerful. This security, stability and dominance you have over your sexuality drives women insane.

Remember this feeling, and remember that you can activate this at any time. You only become more powerful, more attentive as you continue until she screams with pleasure. This is you, always. Feel this feeling, make it yours at this specific moment in time.

WAIT 10 SECONDS

Right now look at yourself from an external point of view. See how you interact with the woman in front of you. You know exactly what to say, you know exactly what to do. Perceive your confidence in every move and realize that it is one of the reasons why she is so attracted to you. Notice how powerful you are, how deeply sensual every thrust of your body is.

You realize that this person who you perceive in your mind is in fact you in every way. Everything you can imagine, everything you can believe is real. This sex god, this master lover that you are depicting is you, it is your inner desires and your unlimited passion. You must only learn to unleash this inside you. Amplify the feeling you are feeling right now and make it yours. Make it become a complete part of who you are.

WAIT 10 SECONDS

You are the embodiment of sexual desire. You understand how to talk to women, how to make them want you more. You have the ability to get inside a woman's mind, to make her dreams come true. You do this naturally as this is part of who you are.

It is easy for you to be sexual, it is easy for you to seduce. Women look deep inside you and know that you will deliver all they expect and more. This is only a side effect of who you are. Allow yourself to be submerged in this idea, allow your body to absorb this feeling. Allow you mind to bind to this sensation right now.

WAIT 5 SECONDS

Right now visualize yourself alone in your master bedroom. Take a moment to fill your presence into the room once more. Make sure that wherever you walk and wherever you look something of yours is reflecting back at this moment. Everything in this place is you and your projections of who you want to be in bed. By now you have felt the deep rising presence of your sexuality, you have seen yourself do pleasurable things to any woman you desire. You have seen yourself in action, on top, being a master at all things sexual. This is not merely a fantasy, this is reality…this is who you really are.

Throughout this entire experience you have actually changed physically and emotionally. You have adopted the projected techniques and now are radiating this strong sense of sexual power. You and all of these images have become one solid entity and you can access this wide pool of sexual energy at will. Take in a deep breath and feel how you are one with this image, one with this moment.

PAUSE 10 SECONDS

As you stand in this room with everything you desire in it, reach out and grab something you can take with you. Something that will create a quick access point back to this place of sexual pleasure and perfection. Take a moment to scan the room and pick up one object small enough to fit in the palm of your hand.

WAIT 5 SECONDS

Now that you have the object in your hands, focus on it and project all that you have seen and experienced into this object. Make a mental note of it and feel the sexual energy radiate from this token. As the feeling intensifies grip the object tightly in your hand. Press it into your skin the moment the feeling peaks. Hold it. Feel how it becomes one with you, how you and this object now share the same connection in space and time.

Whenever you need to access this place of sexual inspiration, of power and confidence simply squeeze your hand and you will be able to access it instantly. This is now your key to enter and go as you please. To turn on or off all your sexual desire at a simply command. You now hold the key in the palm of your hand…you are the key.

USE PREFERRED METHOD TO BREAK THE TRANCE

Passion: A Burning Desire

About the script

This script is for the woman, to feel desirable, deserving of love and to release inhibitions.

Script: Passion: A Burning Desire

USE YOUR PREFERRED INDUCTION METHOD

You are now calm and relaxed, completely safe and sound. You feel warmth surround you completely caressing your body from head to toe. See yourself in a place where you are completely comfortable, where you are absolutely free to express any desire you may have. In this place you are in complete control of every sensation, every thought, every feeling that might arise.

In front of you is a beautiful pond, big enough for someone to completely get wet all over, submerged in water heated to desired perfection. See the vapor slowly rise from the motionless liquid. Feel a strong desire pull you towards the moist pond. You want to get in, you want to feel the water caress your smooth skin all over.

PAUSE FOR 10 SECONDS

Before you can climb into the warm water you must first remove your clothes. As you take off your clothes look at the reflection of your body on the warm water. Notice how perfect and beautiful you really are. See how your breasts radiate sensuality, how your lips call out to be kissed. Notice how perfect your skin is to the touch, how the color of your skin complements every aspect of you.

As you look in this reflection see how attractive you really are. You are absolutely gifted with grace and sensuality. There is no man who can deny you; you are the embodiment of desire. Take this image of you and amplify your sexuality, increase your desirability.

Your eyes seduce, your voice can melt any heart. Your lips are supremely attractive, your tongue can unleash passion with simplicity. Your skin feels like warm silk on those you touch igniting the deepest rawest desire within your partner.

PAUSE 10 SECONDS

Now that you have this perfect imagine of radiant sexuality firmly in your mind begin to approach the warm moist liquid. Let your foot slowly enter into the warmth. Feel the tingling effects of the water climb your legs, to your thighs, your stomach, your breasts, your neck, your face, lips, head. The deeper you enter and the more the water covers your naked body the more intense the feeling of desire becomes. Your sexual needs are deepening. The aroma of the vapor intoxicates you, your insides are all alert, seeking passion and burning for pleasure.

Simply soak yourself and let the water caress your entire body. Allow this desire to seep through your pores, allow it to bond with you. Allow this feeling to become something you can access with a simple thought.

This pool of hot passionate desire can be accessed whenever you wish. You can turn it on at any moment, you are in control.

PAUSE 10 SECONDS

Imagine for an instance that your partner is right in front of you, in this pool of hot moist liquid. Your partner can't resist your sexuality, your absolute beauty. Your security in your body turns your partner on even more. As you engage in blissful sex feel how your souls connect, how your minds and bodies are one. There is no limit to the pleasure you are feeling. Feel every thrust and every touch as an endless moment of pleasure and serenity. The longer you stay the hotter you become the deeper your desire becomes. Remember this feeling right now, this is your pool of desire, this is your place of sensuality. Here you are queen, here you are a goddess of seduction.

PAUSE FOR 10 SECONDS

Once more you are alone in your pond. You feel complete and at peace with your sexuality. You love your body, it's attractive and sexy. As you climb out notice that the perfect reflection you saw earlier is now with you at all times. You have become this pond, you can activate it whenever you decide.

USE PREFERRED METHOD OF BREAKING TRANCE

Part 4: Scripts for Improved Health and Stress Reduction

Cindy's Progressive Relaxation

About the script

Use this script either as an induction, or as a stress reduction/relaxation script. This script and others like it can be useful in conditioning clients to trance and for strengthening ego sensations in clients who are experiencing dissociation due to chronic stress. While it looks to be a short script, the art of this script is in watching and listening to your client carefully during the delivery, and in pacing the delivery in slow, relaxing manner. Highly analytic clients may not respond well to this script, as it may be too slow for their active minds.

Script: Cindy's Progressive Relaxation (Time delivery to 15 minutes)

Begin, as always, by taking a series of deep belly breaths. Breathe deeply, from the abdomen, so that your stomach rises and falls with your breath. Imagine that you're breathing in peace & calm, and that every exhale releases stress and tension. Allow yourself to become more relaxed in your body and mind with each and every breath.

Take a moment to place your body in the best position for relaxation. Take care that your arms are to your sides, palms up or palms down. Have your legs uncrossed, and assure yourself that your body is comfortably supported by the surface you're resting on.

Take another deep breath in, and a long, slow exhale out, as we begin. Close your eyes, if they aren't already, and simply allow all of your attention to rest on the feeling of your breathing, and the sound of my voice.

Consciously release the weight of your body into the support of the surface you're resting on..

Notice how your back makes contact with the support of the surface. If you desire, you can fully contract each muscle group and then relax it, as we move through and relax every muscle group in your body. Fully contracting the muscle (such as making a fist) and then relaxing it, will allow the muscle to relax more completely. However, if you prefer to skip the contraction and simply relax the muscle, that is fine as well.

Begin by relaxing the back of your legs....the back of your hips....your lower back, middle back, and upper back. Feel the weight and relaxation of the back of your body sinking down through the surface you're resting on.

Relax the back of your shoulders / the back of your arms / the back of your neck / and the back of your head. Wiggle and make any adjustments needed to relax the back of your body into the surface more fully. Melt into the support completely.

Now, notice the weight of your body. Notice the weight of your legs, as they rest on the floor. Let your legs be heavy. Let your thighs, feet and toes relax. Release, relax, let go of them completely. Let your legs drift and float and now forget about them.

Notice the weight of your hips and pelvis, as they rest. Let the weight of your pelvis sink into the surface you're on.

Notice the weight of your rib cage. Let the back ribs melt into the support. Feel your abdomen expand with each inhalation. As you exhale, let the belly fully contract. Like a giant balloon inflating and completely deflating. Relaxing deeper with each deep breath.

Notice the weight of your shoulders and arms. Let your arms be so heavy that they sink through the surface you're resting on. Then release them completely. Let go. Let them drift and float away and then forget about them.

Notice the weight of your head. Let the head be heavy. Feel your neck and throat release and relax.

Relax the muscles of your face / relax your eyes and eyelids / your cheeks melt into relaxation / release, relax, let go of your jaw / your forehead and eyebrows smooth and relaxed / feel your scalp melt into relaxation. Your whole head and face totally relaxed, released.

Become aware again of your breathing. Notice each inhalation relaxing the front of your body, and each exhalation relaxing the whole back of your body. Breathing slow, deep and then let it go.

Breathing the body deeper and deeper into relaxation as you drift and float in peace.

Just take a moment to feel how relaxed you are. If you want you can repeat the this process over again, as slowly as you like, or you can just go to any parts of your body that still appear tense, and relax them again.

Deep Healing & Cellular Release

About the script

This script was written when, once again, I could not find a script to fit my client's needs. This script was originally written to accommodate hypnosis in conjunction with massage, but this version has been edited to allow for hypnosis as the sole healing modality. It can, however, be readily used in conjunction with massage, reiki, or other energy healing modalities. I must acknowledge use of some patter from the late Dr. Paul Durbin at the end of this script, which I found to be particularly inspirational and appropriate, and so I have incorporated it here.

Script: Deep Healing and Cellular Release

Surround yourself now with healing energy, the precise healing energy required by your being at this moment in time. Whatever color, texture, transparency, opacity, you imagine this energy as having, the first thing that comes to your mind is right. Imagine this energy with a shape, a color, perhaps a sound, perhaps a feeling--a vibration, a tingle, or as a soft mist. This healing energy has the property of transmuting, that is, as it moves in and through each cell of your body, it has the ability to change blocked energies into energies of beautiful, radiant health. You may you may in the past have experienced these blocked energies as pain, stiffness, injuries, discomfort, and so on, and this healing, transmuting energy changes those energies into vibrant energies of health, and then into healthy tissues. Your own subconscious mind directs and controls this process, just as it directs and controls all the unconscious and non-conscious processes of your being--the rhythmic beating of your heart, the steady flow of your circulation, ... And as your subconscious mind directs and controls this process, you direct and control your subconscious mind, directing it now to release, transmute and heal any and all blocked energies, initiating repair and healing at the cellular level, to bring your body, mind and spirit to a state of ever increasing wholeness, health and light.

As you bring this light in and through your body, your subconscious directs its transmuting energies to the areas of your body that require its healing forces. You can imagine bringing this light energy, this healing force, in through the top of your head and allowing it to flow all the way down and through your body, or you may imagine breathing it in, filling the lungs with the colorful energy and the blood, the circulation, transporting it to every cell, every fiber.

Notice the color of this light, this life force, this powerful transmuting energy, controlled and directed by your imagination, which is the language of the subconscious mind. Notice the color, the intensity; notice the boundaries of this energetic field, how close or far from your body it is. Notice the edges of the field, and you may notice images or flashes of light at the edges of those field, as the healing energy is activated. This is YOUR body's own natural healing power that is emanating here. You can increase it, direct it, focus it; you can allow it to become stronger and to continue to do its perfect, beautiful work, long after this session is over, should you so desire. Because this energy is natural to you, there can be no harm or ill effects as a result of this session, but only beneficial, positive, health-affirming results which can increase and magnify with repeated sessions.

As you experience this session, the physical action of the massage serves to facilitate this process, but it does not create or control it--your own subconscious mind does that. As each area of your body is massaged, you may choose to focus the healing energy into those parts of the body, healing, optimizing, releasing stress and tensions, releasing past events at the cellular level. Or you may choose to trust and allow your subconscious mind to focus the energy where it is most beneficial at this time, secure in the knowledge that your subconscious mind IS your body, and your body IS your subconscious mind. Just as there is no need to consciously direct your heart to beat and your blood to circulate, there is no need to consciously focus this healing energy. The choice is yours, and as you make that choice, you relax even deeper, both physically and mentally. Physically releasing, relaxing, lengthening and softening all muscles, all tendons, opening yourself at all levels to the healing energy that is naturally and rightfully yours, creating the optimal conditions for healing of all tissues at all levels. Healing and strengthening the muscles, healing and optimizing

You may experience this release as a physical sensation, such as a loosening of the muscles and tissues, a softening, a tingle, or in some other way that is appropriate for you. You may experience this release as thought...or memory...or simply a deepening relaxation of both body and mind. However you experience this release, it will be presented to your conscious mind and body in a way that is appropriate, comfortable, peaceful and safe for you at this time.

Continue now bringing the healing, transmuting light into your head...as the light moves into your head, feel and allow your entire being to open to the properties of the light, healing, rejuvenating and restoring your health on a cellular level, restoring the health, the image, the structure of your cells to the perfect blueprint of health and optimal function.

Notice the sensations, be they touch, taste, smell, or something seen or heard. Allow and observe, releasing judgement and opening yourself to the process of perfect healing that only your own subconscious mind can create for you.

As you observe this process, direct and request perfect healing for this area now. Form an image in your mind of this area of your body completely and perfectly healed; functioning at its peak in all areas and in all ways.

PAUSE

Flow the healing light into your neck and as you do so, take a deep breath.

Feel the breath as it enters with a cool feeling and then warming as it gently travels down into the lungs.....

Fill the lungs with a deep inhale, bringing in energy, vitality, healing life force.....

As you exhale, feel the body releasing toxins, stress and any negativity that has accumulated.....

Stay with this breath, focusing on the feeling of deep peace for ten deep inhalations and exhalations....

Feel the energy that is in the body....

Become aware of the warmth and tingling of every cell.....

Feel the energy that is in the extended environment, in every part of nature and in every living thing.....

PAUSE

Now move the healing light down into your shoulders and upper back and let it flow down through your arms all the way into your fingers, and down through the whole of your torso, touching every cell, every nerve, every organ and every gland as it flows through and fills your body with healing, perfect energy.

Visualize or imagine all of that energy shining brightly, as the sun.....

PAUSE

Feel the energy traveling all the way down to your hips.....

Feel it continue traveling down your legs all the way down to your toes.....

Your whole body is now filled with vibrant, vital healing light and energy.....

Allow that healing energy to completely fill any physical area that needs healing energy.....

Feel it warming, healing and expanding through the area......

Allow the healing light to bring peace and healing to any emotional issues or traumas.....

Bring your awareness to any intentions or desires that you may have.....

Hold the thoughts of those intentions or desires as you allow the healing energy to bring your deepest desires to life and your intentions into reality.....

Feel your connection to this healing, perfect energy and light, and know that all is ONE.

PAUSE

Stay with this deep, relaxing, peaceful feeling of bliss.

PAUSE

Now that the healing energy has done its perfect work on the physical level, move the energy into the mental, emotional and spiritual levels. You may imagine riding an escalator up, up up into the clouds or otherwise experience being transported into the higher realms of your consciousness.

Allow the healing light and energy to now join with your higher consciousness as it fulfills its role of aligning your mental, emotional, spiritual and physical healing, healing and perfecting on all levels. In order to facilitate this deep healing on all levels, I am going to ask you to think about certain words or phrases and their meaning for you. I want you to think of these words, to turn them over in your mind, to examine them, to let them sink deeply into your subconscious. Plant them into the fertile soil of your subconscious mind. Imagine a fertile field of grain. You have learned, maybe by living it, maybe by learning in school, that if a farmer plants corn seed, that is what will grow. Now the farmer has to keep the field clean of weeds and grass so that the corn receives the full benefit of the soil. You have to clear the weeds and grass of negative thinking, doubt and fear from the soil of your mind so that these seeds of healing and perfection can grow and work for you.

The first words I want you to think about are the words "good health". What can the words, "good health" mean? They can mean a sense of superb physical well-being with healthy heart and lungs; perfect functioning of all organs, nerves, glands and systems of the entire body; firm, strong muscles, bones and joints; smooth, healthy skin; increased resistance to all forms of infection or disease.

Good health can mean the body feels full of power and strength, with greater balance and stamina, more slender with firm muscle tone in greater awareness of the body, greater control of all parts of the body and sense of harmony in the functioning of the body. Good health may mean less fatigue and illness, and proper body weight.

Good health means that you have overcome habits and behaviors that had a negative influence on your health, and develop good habits that enhance your health, vitality and wellbeing.

Good health means not only physical health, but also a healthy attitude of mind by which your nerves are calm and relaxed. The mind is calm, clear and composed. More tranquil more relaxed, more confident, more secure, and more sure of yourself. You feel better about yourself, happier and more satisfied with your life.

Good health may mean that you have the ability to sleep deeply and soundly when you want to sleep, and then you awake feeling calm, relaxed, confident, cheerful, ready for the activity of the day with energy and enthusiasm. The words "good health" can mean all these things and more. These words have tremendous power. I want you to let them sink deeply into your subconscious mind and let them work for your good health.

The next word I would like you to think about is "success". Success may mean a sense of recognition, a fulfillment of your desires, a sense of accomplishment, an outstanding performance. It may mean a sense of worthiness and attainment of goals.

Success may mean wealthy in terms of money and the things money can buy, or security for yourself and your family. It can also mean

an attitude of mind which gives inner happiness and satisfaction regardless of material possessions or circumstances. It can mean washing away all the blocking energies to set the body's natural healing abilities in motion, creating a healthy body, and a healthy mindset. I want you to use the word "success" to produce in you all the feelings that go with success.

Finally, I want you to think of the word "motivation". It can mean a gradual but progressive change in one's life; to release old recordings of negative habit patterns; to cease to fear being a puppet to one's early conditioning and to become a creator of a new, healthy, happy successful script for your life. It could mean the gradual but progressive building of a stronger and stronger feeling of self-confidence and the ability to meet the challenges of life. It can mean the continual strengthening of your cells through the power of your own mind.

Motivation can mean desire, determination, and a driving force to achieve a desired end. It can mean the desire to take responsibility for your own life and your own health onto yourself, to take charge of your life and success rather than letting life's forces mold and shape your experiences.

We have all been conditioned since birth to associate words with feelings. Words are therefore tools which you are going to use to produce the feeling and results which you want. These words are "good health", "success" and "motivation".

These words are used to improve health, and enable you to be more efficient and effective. This enables you to keep increasing your self-confidence, your self-esteem, you self-reliance, your self-acceptance. Each day you keep improving physically, mentally, emotionally and spiritually. You have a greater sense of your happiness that keeps increasing and you become more enthusiastic and more optimistic each day

Know that you are cleansed, healed and totally purified. Know that your body and the cells in it always strive for a state of perfect health. You are cleansed, purified, healed. Your body's natural state is perfect health. Feel the energy of perfect health flow through you now.

You are energized with good health on all levels - physical, mental, emotional and spiritual. Feel yourself saturated with the energy of good health now.

In closing, feel these thoughts...

May an abundance flow through you on a magnificent scale. May your life be filled with peace, love and prosperity. May you be blessed with good health and loving relationships. Good things are increasingly coming to you and you deserve them!

Made in the USA
Columbia, SC
05 April 2018